WISDOM
FROM
ABOVE
for living here below

LeRoy Eims

While this book is designed for the reader's personal enjoyment and profit, it is also intended for group study. A leader's guide is available from your local Christian bookstore or from the publisher at $2.25.

VICTOR BOOKS

a division of SP Publications, Inc., Wheaton, Illinois
Offices also in Fullerton, California • Whitby, Ontario, Canada • London, England

Foreword

These pages alert the reader to the book of Proverbs as an inexhaustible source of wisdom. Written in lucid style, each chapter provides practical applications of the common sense perspective given in verse after verse.

Out of his personal experience the author shares the significant impact the simple truths of Proverbs have had on his own life. Each succeeding page offers new insight and understanding.

For personal Bible study as well as group sharing, individuals will find this book stimulating and provocative. The pastor as well as the layman involved in Bible study will find this volume profitable reading.

Samuel J. Schultz
Chairman, Division of Biblical Studies
Wheaton College

Second printing, 1978

Library of Congress Catalog Card Number: 77-92704
ISBN: 0-88207-761-9

VICTOR BOOKS a division of SP Publications, Inc.
P. O. Box 1825 • Wheaton, Illinois 60187

Contents

Preface

The person I meet in Asia is generally quiet, thoughtful, meditative, and one who seeks to find meaning in the daily affairs of life. He says, "Give me something deep and spiritual, something that will provide food for my soul and truth for my mind and spirit."

The people I meet in Europe and North America are generally goal-oriented individuals. They say, "Give us something practical, something that will help us face the rough and tumble world as it really is, something to help us in our everyday lives."

I've spent most of my adult life talking to these people about spiritual matters, whether the Asian who wants something spiritual or the Westerner who wants something practical. In either case, I always do the same thing: I hand them a Bible. It meets the needs of both.

One of the Bible's most amazing books is the Book of Proverbs. In various ways it deals with deep spiritual questions as well as with daily practical issues.

This book has emerged from a series of short radio messages I gave on the first nine chapters of Proverbs. It goes out with the prayer that your appetite will be whetted to spend many hours in Proverbs, which reveals the inspired, exciting, and unchanging wisdom of God.

1

Solomon's School of Wisdom

Proverbs 1:1-7

Our world abounds in schools, colleges, and universities. Yet not everyone who wants to enter them for study may do so. The potential student may not have the proper educational background, he may not have enough money, or he may not be able to pass the entrance exam or even the physical.

But everyone is invited to enroll in the school of Solomon. These words are written over its doors: "The young, the simple, the foolish—welcome!" Here the foolish can become wise, and the evil can become good. The wise and the good can become wiser and better.

Those who have studied both the books of Psalms and Proverbs will notice a marked contrast between the two. David, the author of many of the psalms, lived a life filled with danger and war, while Solomon, the author of most of Proverbs, lived a life of peace and quietness. The Psalms reflect the intensity of worship and praise that filled the life of David; the brave and valiant warrior who was constantly being delivered from perils and death by the hand of his faithful God. The Proverbs reflect the quiet study and meditation of Solomon, the man of peace, who had much time to think on the bounty of God and the personal relationship man should have with Him. (See 1 Kings 4:29-30.)

But was his meditation during his reign of peace and quietness the source of his wisdom that had the world talking? Undoubtedly people in all the nations of the Near East had read or heard of his wisdom and knowledge through his prolific writings and sayings. "He spake three thousand proverbs: and his songs were a thousand and five. And he spake of trees, from the cedar tree that is in Lebanon even unto the hyssop that springeth out of the wall: he spake also of beasts, and of fowl, and of creeping things, and of fishes. And there came of all people to hear the wisdom of Solomon, from all kings of the earth, which had heard of his wisdom" (1 Kings 4:32-34).

No, Solomon's wisdom was not simply from meditation, for God Himself was its source. And God had not just looked down from heaven, picked a man arbitrarily out of the crowd, pointed His finger at him, and said, "You're it!" He had answered Solomon's own prayer for wisdom, a prayer that at the time showed a remarkably humble heart. " 'And now, O Lord my God, Thou hast made Thy servant king instead of David my father: and I am but a little child: I know not how to go out or come in. And Thy servant is in the midst of Thy people which Thou hast chosen, a great people, that cannot be numbered nor counted for multitude. Give therefore Thy servant an understanding heart to judge Thy people, that I may discern between good and bad: for who is able to judge this Thy so great a people?' And the speech pleased the Lord, that Solomon had asked this thing" (1 Kings 3:7-10).

Not only was God pleased with this humble request, but He answered it above and beyond what Solomon expected. "Behold, I have done according to thy words: lo, I have given thee a wise and an understanding heart; so that there was none like thee before thee, neither after thee shall any arise like unto thee. And I have also given thee that which thou hast not asked, both riches and honor, so that there shall not be any among the kings like unto thee all thy days" (1 Kings 3:12-13).

What a lesson for us when we have situations in our lives that seem to have no answers—barriers too difficult to overcome—obstacles that are too overwhelming. We also need wisdom. James said, "If any of you lack wisdom, let him ask of God, that giveth to all men liberally, and upbraideth not; and it shall be given him" (James 1:5). God has promised to give wisdom to the person who asks for it.

In the introduction to the Book of Proverbs, Solomon presents his theme, and gives a word of explanation about what he is going to say in this masterpiece of literature which is also the very Word of God.

"The proverbs of Solomon the son of David, king of Israel."

Today's world craves for the sensational, the strange, the unusual, the bizarre. Note, for example, how popular some occult films and books have become. Men seem to have an inordinate desire to penetrate the barrier of the natural, seeking something beyond—the supernatural. Sensationalism is the order of the day in many circles.

Unfortunately churches and Christian groups are not immune to sensationalism. People are sometimes lured to meetings to hear the strange, the unusual, the bizarre. Often it is the testimony of a man or woman who had an unsavory background; the worse it was, the better it will sound and the more people it will attract.

This may have beneficial results. A person may be lured into a meeting on the basis of sensationalism and hear the Gospel proclaimed and be converted to Jesus Christ; he may not have been able to hear it under other circumstances. The headlines got to that person, and he came out of curiosity. Then while he was there, the Holy Spirit spoke to his heart and he surrendered his life to Christ.

But some results are not as good. It can appear to the ordinary Christian, reared in a godly home and converted at an early age, that he cannot be used by God unless he has something grisly to share about his past. He may secretly wish that he had come out of a wild life filled with sin and debauchery or he may even try it for a while so he too could come back to God and boast about his past.

A godly heritage, however, is a blessing from God. Solomon was the son of David, the man after God's own heart. And he was, at least for a while, a wise teacher and leader of his people. Centuries after Solomon's death, Jesus Christ paid an outstanding tribute to him. While trying to help the scribes and

Pharisees understand the reason for His coming, the purpose of His mission, and the truth of who He was, Jesus said, "The queen of the south shall rise up in the judgment with this generation, and shall condemn it: for she came from the uttermost parts of the earth to hear the wisdom of Solomon; and, behold, a greater than Solomon is here" (Matt. 12:42).

God had used two things in Solomon's life to help bring him to a place of usefulness. The first was David's intercessory *prayer* for his son: "Give the king Thy judgments, O God, and Thy righteousness unto the king's son" (Ps. 72:1). David was on his knees before God on behalf of his son, who was to succeed him to the throne of Israel.

This is a tremendous example for us to follow. I have a godly friend whose mother has prayed one hour each day for him since he was born. Well-known author James Dobson and his wife fast for their children one day a week. If you have the care and responsibility for children, don't neglect their spiritual needs. And that means much more than sending them or even taking them to Sunday School and church. It means praying for them fervently day after day, and throughout all of their lives.

The second thing God used in the life of Solomon was the *teaching* of his father. David was a busy man who had many responsibilities, but he did not fail to give godly counsel to his son. In one phase of his teaching he said, "And thou, Solomon, my son, know thou the God of thy father, and serve Him with a perfect heart and with a willing mind: for the Lord searcheth all hearts, and understandeth all the imaginations of the thoughts: if thou seek Him, He will be found of thee; but if thou forsake Him, He will cast thee off forever" (1 Chron. 28:9).

Near the end of his life David reminded his son, "I go the way of all the earth: be thou strong therefore, and show thyself a man; and keep the charge of the Lord thy God, to walk in His ways, to keep His statutes, and His commandments, and His judgments, and His testimonies, as it is written in the law of Moses, that thou mayest prosper in all that thou doest, and whithersoever thou turnest thyself" (1 Kings 2:2-3).

Solomon had the benefit of the godly prayer and counsel of his father. Parents will never regret any time spent on their knees in behalf of their children, or any time invested in teaching them the Word of God. And those who have been raised in such an atmosphere will never regret the godly upbringing they have had.

"To know wisdom and instruction; to perceive the words of understanding; to receive the instruction of wisdom, justice, and judgment, and equity; to give subtilty to the simple, to the young man knowledge and discretion" (1:2-4).

It is really a strange thing when you think about Solomon, the wisest of men, giving instruction to the young and to the simple. It is strange for two reasons. The first is that he *would* do it. In today's academic community, the professor with two or more doctorates normally teaches in a graduate school. This superbrain will give his time to only a few men and women who themselves are working on their master's or doctor's degrees.

But not Solomon. He wrote the first third of this book primarily to the young, and those simple enough to receive instruction. According to Solomon, we should be paying more attention to the formative years of our children's lives, not leaving their key education to the college and university years. Maybe that is what God is trying to tell us in his remarkable book—as the twig is bent, so grows the tree.

The second reason this statement sounds so strange to contemporary ears is that not only *would* Solomon do it, but that he *could* do it. Normally, when a person becomes educated and filled with much knowledge, he finds it difficult to teach the ordinary person. He often talks way over his head. Even some well-educated pastors sometimes have difficulty communicating to their less trained congregations. The spiritual food from the pulpit is sometimes placed on such high shelves that it is out of reach of the beginners.

I was visiting an aircraft plant and one of the vice-presidents was showing me around the premises. As we came to the department for experiments and research, he warned me, "We'll ask these guys a question, but don't worry if you can't understand their answer. Very few people can."

Sure enough, when we talked with these amazingly brilliant

research scientists, we might as well have been talking with some non-English speaking Chinese. These men could not communicate to us at our level.

But this book of Solomon's is able to do just that—communicate to us in simple terms. God speaks to the young and simple and gives them exactly what they need. They who are so easily tricked and deluded *can* know wisdom and instruction, they *can* perceive the words of understanding, they *can* receive instruction in wisdom, justice, judgment, and equity, and they *can* learn the subtlety they need to discern between good and evil, between truth and error. Solomon is able to teach them; he can communicate with them.

Their minds do not have to dance to every new idea that the winds of modern opinion might blow in their direction. They can become men and women of purpose and fixed principle. Their choices, their conduct, and their lives will be governed not by impulse, but by the very wisdom of God.

So you can study this book with that in mind. God can use the Book of Proverbs to keep you on the right road, headed in the right direction. Paul prayed for the Philippians that they would be able to "approve things that are excellent" (Phil. 1:10). He wanted them to have *stability* in the midst of the changing tides of their day. How much more do you need to be on guard in the midst of the waves of divergent opinions that constantly wash up on your shores today—humanism, secularism, materialism, false cults and religions! The Apostle John warned, "Beloved, believe not every spirit, but try the spirits whether they are of God: because many false prophets are gone out into the world" (1 John 4:1). Study this book to keep a firm footing on the solid rock of the truth of God.

"A wise man will hear, and will increase learning; and a man of understanding shall attain unto wise counsels" (1:5).

No one enjoys a wise guy—the person who always has all the answers and is never wrong. He can also be the prankster whose jokes are usually at the expense of others, making them look foolish or embarrassing them in front of their friends.

The wise man in this passage is just the opposite. He listens to people; he knows that he has not arrived. Like Paul, he is still pressing onward for the prize of the high calling of God (see Phil. 3:14). To assume that a person has learned it all is folly and self-deception of the worst kind. "Let no man deceive himself. If any man among you seemeth to be wise in this world, let him become a fool, that he may be wise" (1 Cor. 3:18).

Not much better off than the wise guys are those Christians who feel that God has given them all that He intends to give. It is not that they think they are so wise or great that they cannot change or improve—they know better than that—but they have the false idea that God has revealed all He planned for them. From here on out it is all review and repetition. For them the pastor's sermons and Sunday School discussions do nothing more than cover the same old ground.

At this point in his thinking such a Christian comes to a dangerous plateau of learning, for from then on everything is actually downhill, though he may not realize it. He will lose his spiritual vitality and spark; his walk with the Lord will be bland and tasteless; his life will be filled with the spiritual blahs.

How do you avoid this kind of Christian limbo? The first step is to leaf through the Bible with a view of coming to a new awareness of all that you do not know. Then pray and ask the Lord to give you a real hunger for His Word, and study one topic that you are interested in, something that you may have always wondered about. Get a good concordance and go to work. Look up all the verses that bear on it. This is listening to God and increasing learning.

Many good books give you an abundance of passages on any given topic that you may want to study. Two that I have found helpful in my own life are *The Treasury of Scripture Knowledge* and *Nave's Topical Bible*. (You may get these at your local Christian bookstore.) You can also go to your pastor or Sunday School teacher and ask for ideas that will help you in your personal study.

Now here's a real paradox: the more you learn, the more you will realize there is yet more to learn. The more you know, the more you will realize how much you do not know.

David was a man of the Word and was constantly hungering to know more. "Thou through Thy commandments hast made me wiser than mine enemies, for they are ever with me. I have more understanding than all my teachers, for Thy testimonies are my meditation. I understand more than the ancients, because I keep Thy precepts" (Ps. 119:98-100).

But David was always seeking more. "Open Thou mine eyes, that I may behold wondrous things out of Thy law . . . Teach me, O Lord, the way of Thy statutes; and I shall keep it unto the end. Give me understanding, and I shall keep Thy law; yea, I shall observe it with my whole heart" (Ps. 119:18, 33-34).

The key to increasing learning is to stick to *one thing.* Try to exhaust the topic. Studying everything there is on the subject is the means by which you will grow.

Solomon teaches also the need to listen to wise counsel. People generally will follow a person who knows where he is going. They will also listen to a person who knows what he is talking about, the thrust of the second part of this passage. The Word of God is given so that we might learn how to regulate our affairs and conduct our lives to the glory of God. But we cannot stop there. We are not islands cut off from the needs of humanity; we must roll up our sleeves and lend a hand.

One of the great needs in the church today is that of having wise counselors available to the people. Many are confused in these times; strange voices are heard in the land, luring the people of God into the blind alleys of heresy and false doctrine. Cults abound—old ones and strange new breeds, many from the East. In many instances parents send their children off to school, and when they return their heads are filled with the nonsense spawned by something called "the new morality" and "the greater permissiveness."

Certain seminaries that once rang true and clear in their teaching that the Bible is the very Word of God now produce Christian workers who are not too sure about their foundations. In all this confusion stand the Christians who are earnestly seeking the will of God, but do not know which way to turn, which way to go, and what to do. This makes the need for wise counselors a matter of great urgency.

Note that among the mighty men whom God brought to David was a band of wise counselors. "The children of Issachar, which were men that had understanding of the times, to know what Israel ought to do; the heads of them were two hundred;

and all their brethren were at their commandment" (1 Chron. 12:32). What made these men valuable was that they understood the times in which they lived.

You don't gain that kind of knowledge by reading all the latest novels, by studying all the latest philosophies, or by wasting valuable hours by sitting through the endless variety of films from Hollywood, all supposedly speaking to today's situations. Most of these things simply fill your head with garbage, poison, or chaff.

You gain an understanding of the times as you begin to grasp a knowledge of the needs, hurts, and problems of the people around you. How do you attain to wise counsels? Two things are necessary.

First, become people-oriented. Let your life be open and responsive. Find out what people are thinking by talking to them directly. Solomon said, "A man that hath friends must show himself friendly" (Prov. 18:24). If you do that, people will let down their barriers, open up, and share their lives with you. It is something that friends do.

Second, study the Book of Proverbs. It is filled with ancient wisdom that is good advice for any age. It has something to say to the business executive, to the sinner and the saint, to parents and to children, actually to everyone. One of the ways in which you can study this book is to list the various themes that are dealt with in the book. Start by recording the verses that speak to that theme, and you will be amazed at the wealth of wisdom that you will find.

When you have done that, start sharing with other people, for that which God gives you is not to be clung to selfishly. We are not meant to be reservoirs of knowledge, but channels of blessing. Pray for wisdom and understanding to be a wise counselor in a day in which such counselors are so desperately needed.

"To understand a proverb, and the interpretation; the words of the wise and their dark sayings" (1:6).

Usually the most exciting part of any trip is coming home. To add to the excitement, I generally try to bring a present home to my children as a visible way to demonstrate that I had been thinking of them while I was away. One time I brought a book of riddles home for Randy, our youngest. He was about 10 years old at the time, and for the next two weeks our son entertained the family at the dinner table with his newly learned riddles. He would ask a question, wait with a big grin till we all gave up, and then give the answer and laugh till his sides would ache.

It was a lot of fun for all of us. He would ask things like, "What is white and goes up?"

We'd finally give up.

"A dumb snowflake," he would quip.

"Why is a baseball park so cool?"

And before anyone could guess: "Because there's a fan in every seat.

"If the red house is on the left and the blue house is on the right, where is the White House?

"In Washington, D.C.

"What always falls but never gets hurt?

"Raindrops."

Some riddles in this life, however, are not as funny. Some questions in life seem to have no answers. I was talking with a friend who was having some family difficulties, and there seemed to be no way out of his situation. Whatever he tried only seemed to make matters worse. He told me, "When God finally resolves this situation, I'm going to write a book and call it *What's a Nice Family Like Yours Doing in a Mess Like This?*"

Do you remember the story of the Gordian knot? It was an intricate, complicated knot tied by Gordius, king of Phrygia in Asia Minor. It was so entangled that there was no way it could be untied. Finally Alexander the Great cut it with his sword.

Proverbs will help you gain the kind of wisdom that helps you through the Gordian knots of life. Solomon was famous for being able to find his way through some tough questions. An interpreter for the complicated and difficult things of life is a valuable light in the dark.

One of the values of the education received from Proverbs is that it helps you sift out things worth thinking about. It helps you distinguish between the essential and the trivial. This, in turn, brings security, not the security that comes from doing what others do, but the security based solidly on the truth of the Lord, your personal ideals gained from the ancient wisdom of God.

Much in our world clamors for our attention, effort, and time. Proverbs provides you with wisdom that will help you cut through the complicated knots of life and give you a set of standards to judge the true value of things in the world.

"The fear of the Lord is the beginning of knowledge: but fools despise wisdom and instruction" (1:7).

I once went to an airline desk to check in for a flight to Dallas. The agent at the counter took my ticket, checked the list, and crossed off the wrong name. I smiled, and, as nicely as I could, said, "Excuse me. You crossed off the wrong name. My name is Eims, E-I-M-S. You crossed off Mr. Ellis by mistake."

The agent became quite belligerent, went into a huff, and said, "Well, it looked like Ellis to me. Besides," she continued, "it's no big deal."

"No," I replied, "probably not, until Mr. Ellis shows up."

She didn't like that either. As I sat down to wait for my plane, I thought to myself, *Now what's her problem?* I reflected on it, and then it occurred to me that her problem was most people's problem: we do not like to be corrected. If people are wrong, they do not like to admit it. I don't. If someone shows enough concern to point out a fault or error, people generally do not express their gratitude and thanks. They usually try to justify themselves or argue the point to prove that they are the ones who are right.

This shows up quite early in life. We were having dinner at a friend's house, when our host's eight-year-old began swinging his legs as many kids do when they sit in a chair. The problem was that the son was kicking his dad in the knee. The man laughed, looked at his son, and said, "Hey, pal, watch it! You're kicking your dad in the leg."

The boy frowned, looked at his dad, and replied, "But I just started."

Why do we do that? Why do we try to justify what we do rather than admitting when we are wrong? Why do we despise wisdom and instruction? Probably the greatest single reason is pride. Some of us hate to admit that anyone could possibly be smarter than we are; we're ashamed to acknowledge our ignorance or error. We think that if we do we will be looked on as fools.

But Solomon teaches the very opposite, and that should not surprise us. The wisdom of this world is foolishness with God. It is the normal thing for the world to teach a wisdom that is absolutely contrary to the wisdom of the Word of God. What the world teaches as right is often wrong according to the Scriptures.

For example, situation ethics is the standard of the world these days. Whatever *seems* right to *you,* as you judge it with a mind and conscience contaminated by a sinful nature and a corrupted society, you may freely do. And no one can challenge your actions. Is it any wonder, then, that Solomon says that the wise person *welcomes* instruction—admits when he is wrong, admits that he has needs, admits that he needs help?

This is awfully hard to do. Lila Trotman tells of her early days as the wife of Dawson Trotman, founder of The Navigators. When Dawson would suggest some better way of doing something, she would struggle with an inner rebellion. She did not want to be taught—it took time for her to be willing to learn. Now all of us are like that essentially. We would rather go on in our ignorance than admit that we have a need.

For just this reason, we see the great value of this Book of Proverbs. It is like a great library speaking to us in our many needs. It is awe-inspiring to go into a giant library. There they are: stacks and stacks of books—thousands of them—and more arriving every day. It is incredible to realize that in most of them there is something to be learned. And there are fine libraries all over the world, containing books both old and new.

As you stand before this gigantic mountain of human knowledge, the logical question is, where do you start? Obviously you cannot learn everything, so some things are just going to have to be left to someone else. You don't have the time to master it all. You must get your priorities arranged and put first things first. You cannot afford to major in the minors.

The sensible thing is to figure out what is the most important thing in the world to know and then make sure that you learn that one thing. The Book of Proverbs tells us what that one thing is. Solomon tells us that the fear of the Lord is the beginning, the principal part of true knowledge. Of all things to be known in this world and in this life, this stands at the top of the list. God is to be feared.

What does this expression mean? Some say it means reverential trust, or affectionate reverence. God's love is so beautiful, so tender, so deep and lasting, that it calls forth from our innermost beings a glad desire to do His will and to please Him with our lives.

Let us not forget, however, that when God gave His law to His people, He did so to the accompaniment of thunder and lightning and thick smoke. The people at the foot of Mount Sinai trembled. When we think of the fear of the Lord, let us not eliminate altogether the plain old "being afraid of God." Remember the words of the New Testament, "It is a fearful thing to fall into the hands of the living God" (Heb. 10:31).

The first result of this godly fear is that God must be reverenced for who He is. I have met young people who speak of prayer as "talkin' to the Man upstairs." That is not biblical, for the Bible states clearly that God is not a man (see Num. 23:19). To reverence is to realize and respect the position that a higher authority occupies.

Second, God is to be served. If He is truly Almighty God, if we are His people, if we are living in His Word through a daily experience with Him, it behooves each one of us to find our place of service to Him and joyfully give our lives to the responsibility God has placed before us.

Third, God is to be worshiped. Jesus, in His encounter with the woman at the well of Sychar in Samaria, told her, "But the hour cometh, and now is, when the true worshipers shall worship the Father in spirit and in truth, for the Father seeketh such to worship Him. God is a Spirit, and they that worship Him must worship Him in spirit and in truth" (John 4:23-24).

Fourth, God is to be obeyed. Solomon also wrote, "Let us hear the conclusion of the whole matter: fear God, and keep His commandments, for this is the whole duty of man. For God shall bring every work into judgment, with every secret thing, whether it be good, or whether it be evil" (Ecc. 12:13-14).

Because of all that God has done for us in His grace and

mercy, showered on us in Jesus Christ, we are to love Him with all our hearts, souls, and minds. The Apostle John taught, "We love Him because He first loved us" (1 John 4:19). So when you add it all up, that we should reverence God, serve Him, worship Him, obey Him, and love Him, that is a picture of the beginning of knowledge. And only fools despise it.

The world has gone wrong at this very point. As the psalmist has written of the man of the world, "He flattereth himself in his own eyes" (Ps. 36:2), and he has no fear of God. Solomon says he is a fool.

But as the committed Christian, the disciple of Jesus Christ, seeks to reverence, serve, worship, obey, and love God, he is called a wise person and the blessing of God abides on him. That is what the Book of Proverbs is all about, and that is what it can do for you.

2

The Fervent Appeal of Wisdom

Proverbs 1:8-33

The fervent appeal of the Word of God is for men and women to see and hear, to listen and heed what the Lord has to say to them. That is the essence of wisdom. As Solomon has already said in his introduction, "A wise man will hear" (1:5). The rest of the first chapter further develops that appeal.

First, Solomon vividly portrays the two ways of verse 7 in an earnest fatherly appeal for youth to walk in the way of wisdom and in the fear of the Lord (note the uses of "my son" in verses 8, 10, and 15). Then in the first of a number of passages in which wisdom is personified (1:20-33), an impassioned appeal is made for men to follow her ways (the personification is feminine). In fact, the last verse of the passage is the key statement of the whole section: "Whoso hearkeneth unto Me [wisdom] shall dwell safely, and shall be quiet from fear of evil" (1:33).

"My son, hear the instruction of thy father, and forsake not the law of thy mother: for they shall be an ornament of grace unto thy head, and the chains about thy neck" (1:8-9).

Over the years I have talked with many young men and women who were in trouble. I've sat on curbs and talked with the

19

young nomads who wander from place to place. I've talked with the men in city jails, state penitentiaries, and military brigs and stockades. And I've talked with kids at church meetings who were trying to find their way back. Most of them finally came to the same conclusion, and after much heartache and many tears freely admitted, "You know, I should have listened to Mom and Dad."

The Bible is clear on this principle of obedience to parents. The first commandment with promise was: "Honor thy father and thy mother, that thy days may be long upon the land which the Lord thy God giveth thee" (Ex. 20:12). Some 1,500 years after that declaration Jesus Christ, the Son of God, became our prime example in this matter; though He was the object of worship of all the hosts of heaven, yet on earth He was subject to His parents (Luke 2:51).

Two instructions are given here to youth. First, the young man (or young woman) must listen with a view to obedience. He does not listen to decide whether or not he will respond and do what he has been told to do. He listens as a pupil does to his teacher, as a diligent learner to his instructor. He has already settled in his heart that what he hears will be right, and that his father has his best interests at heart. He knows that his dad wants to help him, give him valuable guidance, and set him on the right path.

Second, he must not forsake the law his mother taught him and exemplified in her life. This is similar to the advice the Apostle Paul later gave Timothy, "Continue thou in the things which thou hast learned and hast been assured of, knowing of whom thou hast learned them" (2 Tim. 3:14).

Today thousands of young men and women are walking the paths of sin and falling prey to all kinds of evil, not because they don't know the way, but because they have forsaken the right paths. Most of them are on the wrong paths because of willful disobedience, particularly to their parents.

Solomon teaches that both parents are to be involved in the training of the child. How often today men pass the buck: "I leave all that religious stuff to my wife. She can make sure the kids get off to Sunday School." The Bible teaches that it is Dad who must also be involved in the training of his children.

Often Dad can get his boy to Little League on time, but

church is considerably farther down on the priority list. He can't find the time; it really isn't that important. The problem is that the son or daughter quickly learns that Dad doesn't consider spiritual things important. And if that is what Dad thinks, then it must be right. Parents must make spiritual things the number one priority in their lives and in the lives of their children.

A godly heritage that results in a godly life is an honor both to the parents and to the child. And like ornaments on the head and necklaces about the neck, that heritage is visible to others. Everyone can clearly see the pleasure of the parents in the child and the honor that child brings to his parents. The Bible speaks of ornaments on the head and chains about the neck as honors bestowed on those who had earned them. Joseph was honored in this way by Pharaoh (Gen. 41:42) and Daniel by the king of Babylon (Dan. 5:29). The Book of Proverbs provides a wealth of instruction to both parents and children alike.

"My son, if sinners entice thee, consent thou not. If they say, 'Come with us, let us lay wait for blood, let us lurk privily for the innocent without cause, let us swallow them up alive as the grave, and whole, as those that go down into the pit; we shall find all precious substance, we shall fill our houses with spoil; cast in thy lot among us; let us all have one purse.' My son, walk not thou in the way with them; refrain thy foot from their path, for their feet run to evil, and make haste to shed blood" (1:10-16).

Every time I read this passage I think of a young man I know. He grew up in a fine Christian family which attended Sunday School and church regularly. During his junior high years he attended a Bible club and really enjoyed it. He was a happy and outgoing young man, had many friends, and was liked by everyone.

Then a strange thing happened during his high school years. He began to hang around a crowd of young people whose life-style was radically different from his. Church had no place in their lives. This group looked on rebellion as a virtue—rebellion against parents, school, society. His hair grew longer, and his interest in the things of God grew shorter; he became more and more fascinated with the lies of the devil and the allurements of the world.

Step by step his life became more and more messed up. He dropped out of school, shifted aimlessly from one thing to another, and finally went into military service. But that didn't work out either. He received an early discharge after having spent most of his enlistment in the brig. He became involved in drugs and the occult, and sin became a total way of life for him. Today he is wanted by the police.

In this passage we note that the first step to sin and degradation is the invitation by this gang of young hoodlums, "Come with us!" (1:11) Isn't it interesting that sinners are so eager to get others to go along with them? But that should not surprise us. When the devil rebelled against God, one of his first acts was to entice Adam and Eve to sin. And that evil has reproduced itself in the human race.

The second step was the invitation, "Cast in thy lot among us!" (1:14) Not only come with us, but now become part of us. Leave your parents, leave your friends, leave your God, leave what you know is right, and become one of us. When that happens, even though there may still be a desire to turn back, it is very difficult to do. It is like trying to stop when you've lost your balance running downhill.

But there is a way to avoid running with the wrong crowd. Solomon says that if sinners entice you, do not consent (1:10). Do not go with them; keep your feet out of their paths (1:15). And the rest of the passage clearly reveals what their goals are and what the results of their evil will be. When Joseph was tempted, he refused the advances of Potiphar's wife and fled. In the words of Moses, "He got him out!" (Gen. 39:12)

Resist the devil and he is defeated; he cannot force you to sin. That choice is yours. Paul encouraged his readers, "There hath no temptation taken you but such as is common to man; but God is faithful, who will not suffer you to be tempted above that ye are able; but will with the temptation also make a way to escape, that ye may be able to bear it" (1 Cor. 10:13).

When we do that—resist temptation—God promises us a place of refuge and protection. The psalmist wrote of God, "Thou art my hiding place and my shield; I hope in Thy Word.

Depart from me, ye evildoers, for I will keep the commandments of my God" (Ps. 119:114-115).

Solomon here warns all of us, young and old alike. There is
not a sin in the catalog of Satan to which the most dedicated
Christian is not susceptible. We must be continually on our
toes and intently obey Peter's admonition, "Be sober, be vigi-
lant, because your adversary the devil, as a roaring lion,
walketh about, seeking whom he may devour; whom resist
steadfast in the faith, knowing that the same afflictions are ac-
complished in your brethren that are in the world" (1 Peter
5:8-9).

The best defense, then, is a good offense. The way to refuse
to go along with the crowd is to have a better alternative. And
that is being in the Word and praying without ceasing. It is
spending time in the presence of God and working for Him.
That and that alone is the life of blessedness and meaning; as
the psalmist said, "Blessed is the man that walketh not in the
counsel of the ungodly, nor standeth in the way of sinners, nor
sitteth in the seat of the scornful. But his delight is in the law
of the Lord, and in His law doth he meditate day and night
(Ps. 1:1-2).

**"Surely in vain the net is spread in the sight of any bird. And
they lay wait for their own blood; they lurk privily for their
own lives. So are the ways of everyone that is greedy of gain;
which taketh away the life of the owners thereof" (1:17-19).**

The course of sin is the course of self-destruction. In this
passage we learn that the greed for gain results in disaster and
calamity. It is difficult for people to understand that there are
things which may appear good on the outside, but which will
eventually be their undoing.

Self-destruction is an illogical mania of much of the human
race. For years the Surgeon General of the United States has
warned that smoking is injurious to health. That warning appears on every package of cigarettes and in their advertising.
The American Cancer Society has campaigned massively, warning people to stop smoking. The American Lung Association
has coined the motto, "It is a matter of life and breath."

Yet in most public places a pall of smoke envelopes smokers

and nonsmokers alike. The world is filled with millions of men, women, and children all puffing away as they travel the path of self-destruction.

Warnings against alcohol have been with us even longer. It has been the cause of numerous broken homes, smashed lives, poverty, and disgrace. The effects of alcohol are clearly seen on any skid row. Medical science calls alcoholism a dangerous disease; we are told that it is hard on the liver and that it befuddles the mind. Drunk drivers kill thousands of people on our roads and highways each year and cause untold damage in lives and property. Yet our magazines are filled with full-page ads proclaiming alcohol's goodness, and bars go on catering to many people who continue to drink.

I was in an air terminal once and was solicited for a contribution to fight alcoholism. When I boarded the plane, we were told that due to a mechanical problem we would be delayed on the ground. But a stewardess then told us in a cheery voice that to compensate for the delay, free drinks would be served to everyone. I thought it strange that in the terminal I was asked for money to help *stamp out* the disease, and on the plane airline personnel were trying to *give* me the disease.

The power behind this drive for self-destruction comes from Satan, the destroyer himself—the enemy of our souls. He wants to destroy man, who is made in the image of God. And there is only one sure weapon against Satan. "Concerning the works of men, by the Word of Thy lips I have kept me from the paths of the destroyer" (Ps. 17:4).

Solomon reminds us that even a bird, when it sees a snare, will not be caught. It has been clearly demonstrated that sin puts the human race on a collision course with destruction. One would think that man would have the sense of a bird and know enough to avoid it. The Book of Proverbs continues to confront man with reality.

"Wisdom crieth without: she uttereth her voice in the streets: she crieth in the chief place of concourse, in the openings of the gates: in the city she uttereth her words" (1:20-21).

One day I visited the grave of my grandfather. As I stood at his burial site, I thought of the generation in which he lived and how it compares to ours. In his day, the world faced a time of turmoil and crisis every decade or so. One country would become upset over another's tariff legislation, things would get tense, and there might even be the threat of war. Then the diplomats would gather and sit down to settle the issues with the cool, calm levelheadedness for which they were noted. A cup of tea, a period of gentlemanly reasoning, a smile, a handshake, a few signatures, and the world went back to another decade of muddling through its normal affairs and problems.

Today, world tension is the norm. If the newscaster does not have some new international blow-up to report, and if he does not come through with a tone of breathless urgency about some matter that could trigger a world catastrophe, we are surprised. Today's man lives in a period of constant global tension.

Besides the tension, today's world is undergoing rapid change. It comes with bewildering regularity. Medical science is always on the verge of a new breakthrough. Operations are now done with laser beams. Something new is always being developed in the fields of communication and transportation. Once I was on a jet and the pilot announced, "Well, folks, the computer tells us our flight time will be two hours and 45 minutes."

As the population increases, technology in agriculture must increase as well. Atomic energy continues to hover in the vague, gray world of being both friend and foe. Dictators continue to threaten the liberty of nations. Wars are commonplace. Our seas are threatened. Our forests and supplies of energy are in danger of being exhausted. Our atmosphere is threatened. Yet in the midst of all these critical problems life goes on.

In light of all these tensions and potential catastrophes, how can a man or woman experience love, joy, and peace as a norm? In a world filled with hate, sorrow, and fear, how can humanity survive? Man cannot escape these problems and crises, so he must learn how to live with them. But the more complex the world becomes, the greater man's need becomes. That is where the wisdom of God must be applied. Human wisdom simply will not suffice. God's wisdom is not only eternal, but also infinite. The puny problems of man are nothing when compared to the manifold wisdom of God.

Most people, of course, have chosen to deny themselves the benefit of this resource of wisdom by turning their backs on God. Man's wisdom, therefore, has led him on a path of unbelievable foolishness. Imagine a drowning man refusing the aid of a lifeguard. Imagine someone lost in the mountains refusing the aid of a rescuer. Imagine a stranded motorist in a howling blizzard refusing a ride to the nearest place of safety. That is the picture of the human race. That is the mess in which humanity finds itself.

But in the midst of this rejection God is not silent. He still calls out to mankind. Solomon personifies wisdom as crying out to men bent on doing things their own way. Thus she is on the outside, calling to humanity. She lifts her voice in the streets—in the highways and byways of life where men are. And she offers them God's way of doing things, God's way of coping with the tensions and crises of life.

Thank God for His Word—which is how wisdom cries out to men today—for it shows us what life can be like, even in the midst of a sinful world. His Word shows us how to find wisdom for ourselves and experience it as a daily reality.

This passage reminds us of the great invitation of Jesus: "In the last day, that great day of the feast, Jesus stood and cried, saying, 'If any man thirst, let him come unto Me and drink'" (John 7:37). Here was Jesus opening His arms, opening His heart to anyone who would come to Him and receive blessing and forgiveness—a whole new life.

As we begin to study the passages in Proverbs that personify wisdom, it will become more and more evident that this personification is of the Person of Jesus Christ. He who was before all things, who is the Alpha and Omega, who is and always shall be, is the very Wisdom of God. Paul tells us that in Jesus "are hid all the treasures of wisdom and knowledge" (Col. 2:3).

In Jesus Christ the floodgates of God's wisdom are opened wide, and this wisdom is made available to mankind through Him as the Word of God. Men are urged to know the truth, the truth of God through Jesus Christ who is Himself the Truth.

The call of God goes out to all men everywhere with an urgency and compassion that is beyond a mere invitation. Jesus Christ as the Wisdom of God cries out in the streets, He cries out in the chief gathering places of men, He cries out where leaders meet, and He sends His words out throughout the cities of men.

That the Wisdom of God is none other than the Person of Christ may be seen in the statement by our Lord, "Therefore also said the Wisdom of God, 'I will send them prophets and apostles, and some of them they shall slay and persecute'" (Luke 11:49). In a parallel passage, Matthew records Jesus saying, "Wherefore, behold, I send unto you prophets, and wise men, and scribes; and some of them ye shall kill and crucify; and some of them shall ye scourge in your synagogues, and persecute them from city to city" (23:34).

He applied the title "the Wisdom of God" to Himself. So it was imperative that the ministry of Jesus be widespread—at the seaside, in the streets, to the multitudes on the mountainsides, in the temple, everywhere He could cast the net of the Gospel—that men and women might be brought into the kingdom of God.

When He gave His disciples their commission on how they were to carry out the ministry, He emphasized that the Gospel should "be proclaimed upon the housetops" (Luke 12:3). God had also reminded His people in the Old Testament, "I have not spoken in secret, in a dark place" (Isa. 45:19). Truth is never ashamed of itself; goodness has nothing to hide. The Wisdom of God goes forth in a loud, clear, ringing tone. The public ministry of Jesus was not carried out in secret or in a dark place.

The epitome of Jesus' work of wisdom was on Calvary's hill —in full view of the crowds. His cross did not stand in a remote part of the wilderness, but in the capital city, at the center of the nation. What He did was heard in the streets, in the chief places of concourse, in the openings of the gates.

"How long, ye simple ones, will ye love simplicity? And the scorners delight in their scorning, and fools hate knowledge? Turn you at my reproof: behold, I will pour out My Spirit unto you, I will make known My words unto you" (1:22-23).

What is a "practical atheist"? He is a person who may claim to believe in God, but lives as though He does not exist. This type of person may go to church, sing in the choir, even teach a Sunday School class, but Monday through Saturday he lives totally for himself. He may hear sermons about the dangers of such a life and may even teach that truth himself, but he's really his own god. That is the kind of person this passage talks about.

Wisdom asks, "How long will you continue in this folly?" But such men continue to ignore the pleading and reproof, and act as though the warnings are only false alarms. They continue in their chosen life-styles, whether these be sinful pleasures, slothful indulgence, or intellectual superiority to the Word of God. They ignore the clear warnings of the Lord. "They consider not in their hearts that I remember all their wickedness; now their own doings have beset them about; they are before My face" (Hosea 7:2).

Here are three classes of people. The first are the simple ones. These are people who are easily influenced either for good or evil. During the late 1960s and early 1970s we witnessed the spectacle of thousands of young men and women being lured into the false religions of the East. Other thousands fell for the false promises of the drug culture.

The second group are the scorners, who pride themselves in their own intellectual achievements and mock that which is holy and good. These are the proud, arrogant men who lead the simple ones astray. The psalmist speaks of these: "Hide me from the secret counsel of the wicked; from the insurrection of the workers of iniquity, who whet their tongue like a sword, and bend their bows to shoot their arrows, even bitter words, that they may shoot in secret at the perfect. Suddenly do they shoot at him, and fear not. They encourage themselves in an evil matter; they commune of laying snares privily; they say, 'Who shall see them?' They search out iniquities; they accomplish a diligent search" (Ps. 64:2-6).

They pride themselves on the fact that they do not need God. And they even look down at those who do, as though they are people needing a crutch. To them the need for Christ is a sign of weakness that is to be shunned by intelligent people.

The last group are the fools who hate knowledge. Obviously a person who hates knowledge is a fool. Knowledge helps make a person wise, but the greatest wisdom is the Word of God which is able to make him wise unto salvation through faith which is in Jesus Christ.

A sailor had recently come to Christ. He was standing on the deck of his ship one morning reviewing some Scripture memory verses that were printed on small cards. Another sailor approached him and asked, "What are you looking at? Dirty pictures?"

It just so happened that the Bible verses the Christian was reviewing were John 3:19-20. So the sailor smiled, handed the card to his shipmate, and replied, "Yeah, isn't that the dirtiest picture you have ever seen?"

That passage states, "And this is the condemnation, that light is come into the world, and men loved darkness rather than light, because their deeds were evil. For everyone that doeth evil hateth the light, neither cometh to the light, lest his deeds should be reproved."

That's the problem with the simple ones, the scorners, and the fools—sin. What is the solution? They must repent and turn to God. Isaiah put his finger right on it when he said, "Hear the Word of the Lord, ye scornful men" (Isa. 28:14). The Scriptures, believed and applied, are the answer to the needs of these three classes of men who are headed for destruction. These three groups are called to repentance.

Often, people who have lived in sin, who have hated the knowledge of God, and who have mocked the way of righteousness say that they are too set in their ways to be able to turn around and begin a whole new direction. That could very well be in human strength alone, but God makes some tremendous promises to those who desire to change. Those people will be given the help of the Holy Spirit and the strength and enlightenment of the Word of God.

Is repentance or completely changing one's way possible apart from the Holy Spirit? Not according to the Bible. No man can turn to God through his own efforts. But the point is that he does not have to. If a person senses in his own soul the stirrings of desires to leave his old ways, the Holy Spirit is already at work in that life. God meets man more than halfway. God does not say here that He will send His Spirit to influence men in some small and insignificant way. He says, "I will pour out My Spirit unto you." God will give more than is needed to show how to come to Him. He will do more than His share, both to will and to do that which men could not do in their own strength.

The second thing a person needs in coming to God is some clear instruction, which God also promises to give. "I will make known My words unto you." What a tremendous thing it is to have the living and true God ready, willing, and eager to teach us His precious Word.

The wisdom of the Scriptures is made alive by the Holy Spirit. Jesus Christ, the Living Word, infuses Himself into the written Word. "It is the Spirit that quickeneth; the flesh profiteth nothing; the words that I speak unto you, they are spirit, and they are life" (John 6:63).

But the man who hardens himself against the knowledge of God finds the Word of God a closed book, not because the Word is dark and difficult, but because man is. The Word of God is light itself. But the man who rejects it is living in the darkness of rebellion and sin. His mind, his will, his appetites, his soul, everything about him is cut off from the light. "The natural man receiveth not the things of the Spirit of God, for they are foolishness unto him, neither can he know them, because they are spiritually discerned" (1 Cor. 2:14).

The commission of Jesus to Paul is highly significant in light of that. Paul was sent to the multitudes living in sin "to open their eyes, and to turn them from darkness to light, and from the power of Satan unto God, that they may receive forgiveness of sins, and inheritance among them which are sanctified by faith that is in Me" (Acts 26:18).

Even the weakest response will be received and blessed by God. The promise and warnings go hand in hand. " 'Come now, and let us reason together,' saith the Lord, 'though your sins be as scarlet, they shall be as white as snow; though they be red like crimson, they shall be as wool. If ye be willing and obedient, ye shall eat the good of the land, but if ye refuse and rebel, ye shall be devoured with the sword; for the mouth of the Lord hath spoken it' " (Isa. 1:18-20). Man's feeble response is fully met by the great and powerful grace of our merciful God.

But he also asks, "How long are you going to wait?" Delay is folly. Do not resist the Holy Spirit, for God's Spirit will not always strive with man. Paul stated, "Behold, now is the accepted time; behold, now is the day of salvation" (2 Cor. 6:2).

"Because I have called, and ye refused, I have stretched out My hand, and no man regarded. But ye have set at nought all My counsel, and would none of My reproof; I also will laugh at your calamity; I will mock when your fear cometh; when your fear cometh as desolation, and your destruction cometh as a whirlwind; when distress and anguish cometh upon you. Then shall they call upon Me, but I will not answer; they shall seek Me early, but they shall not find Me; for that they hated knowledge, and did not choose the fear of the Lord; they would none of My counsel; they despised all My reproof. Therefore shall they eat of the fruit of their own way, and be filled with their own devices" (1:24-31).

This passage is one of the clearest in Scripture of the *fact* of God's judgment and the *reason* for His judgment. He has called, and His call has been refused. Possibly you are one of those to whom the call of God came, but you have not responded. And you might even have an excuse, "I have never heard the call of God; God has never spoken to me." That may be, but what probably has happened is that God has called, but you refused to listen.

How does God call? First of all by His Word. "Come unto Me" is a cry that is echoed throughout the Bible. He calls for us to turn to Him. He asks, "Why will ye die?" He invites, "Whosoever will, may come." His Word is carried by His ministers from pulpits and by His people door to door as the church fulfills its responsibilities in evangelism. Gospel tracts may be found in hotel lobbies, airline terminals, and bus and train depots. Radio and TV carry the Gospel message. Missionaries cover the globe with the Gospel of Jesus Christ. Bibles abound in hotel and motel rooms around the world, and are for sale in bookstores, department stores, supermarkets, and discount stores.

God's call goes out in other ways as well. The circumstances of life, either good or bad, have been used of God to influence thousands for Christ. Man's own conscience often leads him to inquire into spiritual matters. By a multitude of other means the call has gone forth, but often to no avail. Man has, on the whole, disregarded the outstretched hand of God.

This is an amazing thing. Here is the King of the universe, worshiped by the adoring hosts of heaven, reaching out and pleading, calling on sinners to turn and walk with Him. Yet His counsel and reproof are set at naught.

But there is a day coming when all of that will be changed. The day of grace is still here; the door of salvation still stands open. There is still time to repent and turn to God. But one day it will be too late. The obituary columns of the newspapers of the world daily record the passing of thousands into eternity. When you become one of those statistics, will you be ready?

Also, one day the Lord will bring this earthly drama to an end. "For the Lord Himself shall descend from heaven with a shout, with the voice of the archangel, and with the trump of God; and the dead in Christ shall rise first. Then we which are alive and remain shall be caught up together with them in the clouds, to meet the Lord in the air; and so shall we ever be with the Lord" (1 Thes. 4:16-17). The dead in Christ will be with Him forever.

But for those who do not know God that will be a day of desolation, distress, destruction, and anguish. Though an attempt at excuses will be made, it will be too late. The fruit of sin is its own reward. The sinner reaps what he has sown. God, who has been refused, disregarded, hated, and mocked, will let man proceed on his own chosen path. He will no longer have to pass by the spectacle of God's only begotten Son suffering on the cross for his sins. The road to a Christless eternity will open wide with no signs posted on it to show how to turn around and head for heaven. The opportunity for choice will be gone.

The writer to the Hebrews expressed it vividly: "If we sin wilfully after that we have received the knowledge of the truth, there remaineth no more sacrifice for sins, but a certain fearful looking for of judgment and fiery indignation, which shall devour the adversaries. He that despised Moses' law died without mercy under two or three witnesses; of how much sorer punishment, suppose ye, shall he be thought worthy, who hath trodden under foot the Son of God, and hath counted the blood of the covenant, wherewith he was sanctified, an unholy thing, and hath done despite unto the Spirit of grace? For we know Him that hath said, 'Vengeance belongeth unto Me, I will recompense,' saith the Lord. And again, 'The Lord shall judge His people.' It is a fearful thing to fall into the hands of the living God" (Heb. 10:26-31).

"For the turning away of the simple shall slay them, and the prosperity of fools shall destroy them. But whoso hearkeneth unto Me shall dwell safely, and shall be quiet from fear of evil" (1:32-33).

Let's just suppose that you have moved to a new town and the chairman of the Chamber of Commerce meets you. He tells you that if you live on this side of the river, your home will be absolutely safe. You will not have to fear thieves or robbers; you can leave your doors unlocked, leave your keys in the car, and walk the streets at night safely. Your home, furthermore, will be safe from fire, flood, and storms.

On the other side of the river, he says, it is just the opposite. Dangers lurk everywhere. Tornadoes, hail, and earthquakes are common. The fire trucks are always busy; the police constantly have their hands full. Muggings are common, and all the people live in constant fear of natural disasters, criminals, disease, and death. If you had your choice, in which part of this town would you choose to have your home?

Strangely enough, in the matter of the eternal soul, most people make the wrong choice. God categorically promises that whoever listens to Him will be safe and free from evil, but most people just do not believe Him.

The psalmist described such men vividly, "Therefore pride compasseth them about as a chain; violence covereth them as a garment. Their eyes stand out with fatness: they have more than heart could wish. . . . They set their mouth against the heavens, and their tongue walketh through the earth. . . . And they say, 'How doth God know? And is there knowledge in the most High?' " (Ps. 73:6-7, 9, 11)

One morning I was in an elevator with two young men. Their language was loud and filthy. One was wearing a large belt buckle on which obscene words were cast in bronze for all to see. They were going forth into a day which both hoped would satisfy their greed and lusts. Nothing mattered in this world to them but the gratification of their polluted desires. They were plunging headlong down the trail to destruction and no one or nothing was going to be allowed to stop them. They had turned away to the way of death.

In other parts of that city and in all the places of the world other men were doing the same. Some were dressed in well-tailored suits and carried briefcases filled with important papers; they drove expensive and luxurious cars. Their looks and manners were different from the two young men in the elevator, but their intent was the same—the fast buck, ill-gotten gain, their minds consumed by greed and lust.

Does it really matter what takes us away from God? Of course not. The violent passions of youth, the quiet respectability of maturity, the relaxed years of old age—if the heart is turned to that which cements our affections to this world, we are in grave danger.

But consider the opposite. God gives a great promise to the one—whether he or she be young, middle-aged, or elderly—who listens to Him. That person will dwell safely under the shadow of the Almighty, and will have no evil to fear.

The option is clear: destruction or safety. And this is the day to choose. For that is the fervent appeal of wisdom—choose now.

3

Wisdom Is God-given

Proverbs 2:1-9

Solomon has spent a great portion of chapter 1 of the Book of Proverbs warning the scorner, the foolish, and the rebellious. He has not painted a pretty picture for them. The deserved end of these people is their destruction. God is making an appeal to these, who have turned away, to come back to Him. God is "not willing that any should perish, but that all should come to repentance" (2 Peter 3:9).

Solomon is convinced that "a wise man will hear" (Prov. 1:5), and through the Holy Spirit even the simple can become wise, even the scorner can come to Him, even the rebel can repent and return, as did the prodigal son. The first nine verses of chapter 2 develops that theme. That section has to do with seeking God, receiving His truth, and gaining understanding of His ways.

"My son, if thou wilt receive My words, and hide My commandments with thee; so that thou incline thine ear unto wisdom, and apply thine heart to understanding; yea, if thou criest after knowledge, and liftest up thy voice for understanding; if thou seekest her as silver, and searchest for her as for hid treasures; then shalt thou understand the fear of the Lord, and find the knowledge of God" (2:1-5).

35

Solomon now turns his attention to those who have a heart to learn and grow, to obey and serve. Centuries before, Job had asked the question, "But where shall wisdom be found? And where is the place of understanding?" (Job 28:20, literal translation) Even now, the cry of Pontius Pilate can be heard as it echoes down the corridors of time, "What is truth?" (John 18:38) In this section these questions are answered; the subjects of what wisdom actually is and how one may get it are discussed.

The passage is a complex conditional clause, "If . . . then . . ." *If* a person does certain things—the three "if" clauses of verses 1-4—*then* certain things will be true of his life (v. 5). So it is important for the person who would receive understanding and knowledge to do six things.

The Word of God. The first step is to receive the Word of God. Many Scriptures instruct us on what that means. In the parable of the sower, for example, Jesus spoke of those who with "an honest and good heart, having heard the Word, keep it and bring forth fruit with patience" (Luke 8:15). Mary, the sister of Martha and Lazarus, typifies this spirit, for she "sat at Jesus' feet, and heard His Word" (Luke 10:39).

The Apostle Paul brought God's Word to many people, groups, and churches. Among these the Bereans have stood out as good examples, for they "were more noble than those in Thessalonica, in that they received the Word with all readiness of mind, and searched the Scriptures daily, whether those things were so" (Acts 17:11). They are commended in the Bible because of their responsive hearts and positive attitudes toward the Word.

Though the Bereans were commended above the Thessalonians, the latter also had received the Word in the right way: "For this cause also thank we God without ceasing, because, when ye received the Word of God which ye heard of us, ye received it not as the word of men, but as it is in truth, the Word of God, which effectually worketh also in you that believe" (1 Thes. 2:13).

The Word of God, therefore, must not be received as a stranger at the door, but as a friend whom we have been longing to see, as a teacher for whom we have the greatest respect and from whom we are eager to learn, and as a wise counselor on whom we can lean for advice and direction in life.

Scripture Memory. The second instruction to those eager to be taught is to memorize Scripture, to "hide [God's] commandments with thee." This means that we lodge the Word of God in our hearts so that it might ever be with us. It is one of the greatest blessings and most profitable spiritual exercises in which we can engage.

I began this practice as a young Christian. I was working at the Sears store on Lake Street in Minneapolis, and I walked 10 blocks to and from work. I used that time to memorize Scripture. I had enrolled in The Navigators *Topical Memory System,* and the verses were sent to me on small cards that I could carry wherever I went. I memorized scores of verses and reviewed them diligently. To this day I can recall those verses, and frequently in a witnessing situation the Holy Spirit brings one or more to my remembrance. Time that could easily have been wasted was put to good use as I stored the Word of God in my heart. Those 20 blocks I walked each day became a time of tremendous spiritual growth that has proved its value to me over the years. Once the Word of God is securely placed in the heart, Satan cannot snatch it away.

Attentive Listening. The third key to unlocking the mystery of how to become a man or woman of wisdom and understanding is to incline the ear to wisdom. What does that expression mean? What is Solomon getting at?

If you've ever attended a concert, you have noticed that some people are listening intently, while others are not. Some are interested and some are not. Those who like classical music are sitting there, caught up in the wonder of it all, enraptured by the thrill of hearing highly motivated and trained musicians give their all. But others in the audience are bored stiff; they would rather be somewhere else doing what interests them.

A woman told me about taking her husband to the opera, which she loved very much. From time to time during the performance she would glance at her husband trying to discern his reactions. To her surprise he was sitting there with a placid expression. She was charmed by the idea that her husband, whom she fully expected to hate every minute of it, actually seemed to be enjoying himself. But on closer investigation, she discovered that he had an earphone on and was listening to the ball game on his small transistor radio!

Inclining the ear to wisdom means listening attentively to what God has to say, eagerly sitting on the edge of our chairs, so to speak, not wanting to miss anything He has for us.

Obedient Application. The fourth step is to apply our hearts to understanding. To listen attentively to the Word of God with no intention of obeying its truths or following its instructions is to listen in vain. The point of applying our hearts to understanding is that our hearts and lives might be affected by what God says.

Two keys to this are a realization of our own needs and an awareness of who is speaking when we read the Bible. We need to realize, first of all, that we are unable to find the way by ourselves, and need the help of God. Without Him life remains a confused plot filled with unanswered questions. We need to know that we need Him.

We must also realize that it is God Almighty who is speaking to us through the Word. He is the Creator of heaven and earth, the sea and all that is in them. His primary intent is not to increase our knowledge of the Bible, but to help us become better Christians, to affect our lives, and to mold us more and more into the image of His Son, the Lord Jesus Christ.

It is the application of the Word of God to the heart, not merely the understanding of the Word with our minds that is so necessary. Naturally we cannot do the truth and live the truth unless we know the truth, but all too often we stop there. We are content to learn something without the follow-through of application. Both are the ministry of the Holy Spirit who will illumine the Word of God to our minds and hearts.

Persistent Prayer. In the fifth step in the search for wisdom, knowledge, and understanding, Solomon turns to the matter of prayer. He places it before the acts of seeking and searching (Prov. 2:4). In the teachings of Jesus, the same order is followed: Ask God and it shall be given you, then seek and you will find (see Matt. 7:7).

As we incline our ears to the wisdom of God and apply our hearts to understand it, we must be in the proper spirit of prayer. Only then can the Holy Spirit sensitize our consciences and enlighten our spiritual understanding. The knowledge of this world can be gained by diligent study in the field of education; the knowledge of God is gained only as our study of God's Word is permeated with prayer.

A person can become a Bible scholar through study alone. But is that the objective men should have in life? To have a good knowledge of the Bible? No, the goal Christians should have is to know God. Naturally we must study the Scriptures if we are to come to a deeper understanding of God and His ways, but the time we spend in the Book must be saturated with prayer.

Yes, you *can* learn the Bible by study alone, but you cannot become a spiritual Christian, a man or woman of God, without engaging in *both* study and prayer. Through prayer, the Word that enters our minds through our ears and eyes sinks down into our receptive hearts. And our lives are definitely changed by it.

The Word of God is like a great treasure house of spiritual truth. The door is fastened by a number of locks that guard its precious truths from the halfhearted and from those who are merely curious but have no real spiritual hunger or intent to apply its words to their hearts. Prayer is the first key that must be inserted, in the divine order of things, to open up the riches of God's Word. It is equivalent to the prayer of the psalmist, who said, "Open Thou mine eyes, that I may behold wondrous things out of Thy law" (Ps. 119:18).

One of the greatest blessings I have experienced has been the practice of praying over the Word verse by verse. This has been true in meeting the needs of my own heart and a powerful means of helping another Christian who is finding it difficult to follow the Lord. Specific needs can be met through prayer, without much counsel or discussion.

I recall a young man who was always getting himself into trouble by some slip of the lip. One day we sat down for some fellowship, and I suggested we pray over the third chapter of James. We took the time to pray over it verse by verse. I prayed over one verse, and he over the next, and so on through the chapter. God, through the Holy Spirit, spoke to his heart in a dynamic and dramatic way. It was the turning point in his life in gaining victory over his tongue. Had we merely *discussed* the passage, not much would probably have happened;

but when we prayed over it—cried out and lifted up our voices—the truth sank deeply into his soul.

Diligent Study. The sixth word of instruction is for us to go on a mining expedition. Mining was an ancient art, for even Job spoke of it: "Surely there is a vein for the silver, and a place for gold where they fine it. Iron is taken out of the earth, and brass is molten out of the stone" (Job 28:1-2).

Ruins have been found of ancient copper mines in the Sinai Peninsula and gold mines in the desert of Egypt which were there long before the time of Solomon. The Bible states that "all the kings of Arabia and governors of the country brought gold and silver to Solomon" (2 Chron. 9:14).

But mining was not the only activity that led men of ancient times to search for treasure. Rich men would often bury their wealth in the earth to keep it safe. And frequently they would die without revealing the place it was hidden. So the treasure hunt is a practice of great antiquity among the people of the Near East.

The Lord Jesus Christ in His ministry often made reference to this practice in teaching about the kingdom of heaven. "Again, the kingdom of heaven is like unto treasure hid in a field; the which when a man hath found, he hideth, and for joy thereof goeth and selleth all that he hath, and buyeth that field" (Matt. 13:44).

Solomon uses the treasure picture to point out an important truth. The knowledge of God does not come through prayer alone. The devotion of prayer is no substitute for the diligence of study. The two go hand in hand. In order for us to know the mind of God, to be directed in His way, to know how to bring honor and glory to His name, to serve the Lord in the way that is acceptable to Him, we must not only ask in prayer, but seek and search the Scriptures in patient and unhurried study. Prayer comes first, but it is the means by which God energizes our study efforts and makes the results rich and rewarding.

Solomon is not speaking here about reading the Bible. This, of course, is a worthy and necessary means of getting into the Word. Here, however, Bible *study* is commended. Bible reading merely scratches the surface, while Bible study gets us beneath that upper layer to the sacred storehouse of the truth of God.

And the truths that are buried there are withheld from the hurried and superficial reader.

In the gold fields of Colorado one can still see the remains of the great mines that once flourished in magnificent mountain splendor. As you explore these old mines, you become aware that any discovery near the surface only spurred the miners to greater and deeper search. They were looking for the mother lode, that great vein of gold that was hidden far beneath the surface.

In this passage Solomon tells us what that priceless treasure is. The one who seeks and searches will learn the fear of the Lord, which is the beginning of wisdom, and find the knowledge of God, which is the final and ultimate discovery of the human heart. Jesus said that He came to this earth to reveal the truth of God in all its fullness. He stated, "And this is life eternal, that they might know Thee the only true God, and Jesus Christ whom Thou hast sent" (John 17:3).

Years later, the Apostle Paul prayed for the Ephesian church: "That Christ may dwell in your hearts by faith; that ye, being rooted and grounded in love, may be able to comprehend with all saints what is the breadth, and length, and depth, and height; and to know the love of Christ, which passeth knowledge, that ye might be filled with all the fullness of God" (Eph. 3:17-19). This prayer can be answered in our lives as we diligently apply ourselves to the patient and regular study of God's Word.

If these six conditions are met—receiving the Word of God, memorizing it, deliberately being attentive to it, applying it to our lives, praying for wisdom, and diligently studying it—then we shall know how to reverence God aright and gain true knowledge of Him.

"For the Lord giveth wisdom: out of His mouth cometh knowledge and understanding" (2:6).

After presenting the conditions for successful living, Solomon gives a word of explanation about how we can be kept from error. Jesus put His finger on the root cause of falsehood and error in spiritual matters when He said, "Ye do err, not knowing the Scriptures" (Matt. 22:29). History bears no record where a turning away from the faith resulted from a humble, honest, prayerful, diligent study of the Word of God.

Solomon teaches an important truth here: God gives wisdom. Wisdom is a gift from God, but God reserves this gift for those who demonstrate by their time in the Word that they truly desire it. And the great and precious promises of God show us clearly that we will never search in vain. "Thus saith the Lord, thy Redeemer, the Holy One of Israel; 'I am the Lord thy God which teacheth thee to profit, which leadeth thee by the way that thou shouldest go'" (Isa. 48:17). Wisdom, like every other good and perfect gift, "is from above and cometh down from the Father of lights, with whom is no variableness, neither shadow of turning" (James 1:17).

The life of Daniel the prophet illustrates this point. His personal safety was on the line because he had promised the powerful king of Babylon that he could reveal what the king had dreamed and subsequently forgotten. All the wise men, the magicians, the astrologers, the sorcerers, and the Chaldeans had been called on to do so but they all failed.

Daniel asked his three friends to meet with him to pray about the problem. "Daniel went to his house, and made the thing known to Hananiah, Mishael, and Azariah, his companions: that they would desire the mercies of the God of heaven concerning this secret; that Daniel and his fellows should not perish with the rest of the wise men of Babylon. Then was the secret revealed unto Daniel in a night vision. Then Daniel blessed the God of heaven . . . and said, 'Blessed be the name of God for ever and ever: for wisdom and might are His. . . . I thank Thee, and praise Thee, O Thou God of my fathers, who hast given me wisdom and might, and hast made known unto me now what we desired of Thee, for Thou has now made known unto us the king's matter'" (Dan. 2:17-20, 23).

Daniel was a man of prayer, but he was also a man of the Word. Later in the book you find him diligently studying the writings of Jeremiah. "In the first year of his reign I Daniel understood by books the number of years, whereof the Word of the Lord came to Jeremiah the prophet, that he would accomplish seventy years in the desolations of Jerusalem" (Dan. 9:2). Prayer and diligent study of God's Word have always been the hallmark of great men of God throughout the ages.

Think for a moment of all the wise men of the earth. Who among them can give you wisdom? None of them. Not one can impart wisdom to you or to any other human being. They can make an earnest effort to teach you what they know, but that is not the same. In the universities around the world today there are students who are passing their courses and others who are failing. That would not be true if the instructors could give their wisdom to their students. But they cannot. They can make it available, explain it, repeat it, but they cannot give it. Only God can do that. "If any of you lack wisdom, let him ask of God, that giveth to all men liberally, and upbraideth not; and it shall be given him" (James 1:5).

God is wisdom. God has wisdom. God is ready and willing to give you that wisdom if you will meet the conditions He has laid out in His Word. Out of His mouth, through the writings of holy men of God moved by the Holy Spirit, He has given us His Word. That is the revelation of His knowledge and understanding. Beyond the shadow of a doubt, the greatest gift ever bestowed on the human race—apart from the salvation wrought by Jesus Christ, the living Word—is the Holy Bible, the written Word.

"He layeth up sound wisdom for the righteous: He is a buckler to them that walk uprightly. He keepeth the paths of judgment, and preserveth the way of His saints" (2:7-8).

Not only is God the Author and Giver of wisdom, but He stores it up for the upright. This points up the contrast of the wisdom of God and the wisdom of this world. Solomon, in another book, spoke of the wisdom that most people base their lives on: " 'Vanity of vanities,' saith the Preacher, 'vanity of vanities; all is vanity.' . . . I have seen all the works that are done under the sun; and, behold, all is vanity and vexation of spirit. . . . And I gave my heart to know wisdom, and to know madness and folly: I perceived that this also is vexation of spirit. For in much wisdom is much grief: and he that increaseth knowledge increaseth sorrow. . . . And moreover I saw under the sun the place of judgment, that wickedness was there; and the place of righteousness, that iniquity was there" (Ecc. 1:2, 14, 17-18; 3:16).

Here is vanity, vexation, grief, sorrow, wickedness, and iniquity. The Apostle Paul adds another dimension, "The wisdom of this world is foolishness with God" (1 Cor. 3:19). James describes human wisdom as "sensual, devilish" (James 3:15).

But here Solomon speaks of "sound wisdom." In contrasting this earthly wisdom James wrote, "But the wisdom that is from above is first pure, then peaceable, gentle, and easy to be intreated, full of mercy and good fruits, without partiality, and without hypocrisy" (James 3:17). The major question, then, is this: Who is eligible to receive the wisdom from God? The answer is readily given: the righteous. They are those who have been clothed with the righteousness of Christ Himself.

The Bible is a Book whose Author you have to know before you can understand it and receive its benefits and claim its great and precious promises. The truth of God is spiritually discerned. So the man or woman who enjoys the indwelling and illumination of the Holy Spirit is the one to whom the Bible makes sense.

Time and again you hear testimonies of people to whom the Bible was a closed Book—a mystery and a puzzle—before they were born again into the family of God. After they came to Christ, they found the Scriptures to be a rich blessing to their lives each time they opened it and read its pages. It was so interesting, helpful, and meaningful that they could hardly put it down.

This passage goes on to give insight into another facet of the goodness of God to His people. He not only imparts sound wisdom, but provides protection for them. The psalmist wrote, "Thou art my hiding place and my shield; I hope in Thy Word" (Ps. 119:114). What a precious privilege is ours when we walk with the Lord. He is our protection at all times, so that we can say with David, "The Lord is my rock, and my fortress, and my deliverer; my God, my strength, in whom I will trust; my buckler, and the horn of my salvation, and my high tower" (Ps. 18:2).

This protection is expressed in three statements which should greatly encourage the child of God. God promises to be a shield to those who walk uprightly. He is their protection against all enemies. This aspect of God's directly protecting power is seen in His promise to Abraham, "I am thy shield, and thy exceeding great reward" (Gen. 15:1); in many psalms God is a shield to His people (Ps. 33:20; 84:11; 91:4; 144:2). And those who walk uprightly are those who walk in the ways of God.

Second, God keeps the paths of those who walk justly (Prov. 2:8, literal translation). The phrase "the paths of judgment" is an expression that means the paths of the just or the paths in which the just walk. God watches over all the ways His people walk, and guides, superintends, and protects them. And the just are those who are clothed in the righteousness of Jesus Christ.

Third, God preserves the ways of all His saints. This thought is similar to the expression of the psalmist that God "suffereth not our feet to be moved" (Ps. 66:9), and Hannah's faith that God "will keep the feet of His saints" (1 Sam. 2:9). The saints, God's "holy ones," are ever under the watchful care and protection of the Lord. They are men and women who understand the fear of the Lord and have found the knowledge of God.

"Then shalt thou understand righteousness, and judgment, and equity; yea, every good path" (2:9).

Solomon gives an all-important promise to those who will study the Word of God and pray over it. An understanding will be given of three important matters that are absolutely essential if the world is to live in peace and harmony.

The first is *righteousness*. This is a word that is alive with meaning. In our standing before God it means the perfect holiness of Jesus Christ which God imputes to us when we embrace the Lord Jesus as our own personal Saviour and Lord. But it also has a vital meaning in our relationship with our fellowmen. It means acting in a just and upright manner, doing what is right and virtuous.

In the mid-1970s the news media was filled with reports of cheating, scandals, political wrongdoing, underhanded financial deals in government—nationally and internationally—and immoral escapades in high places. If *righteousness* had been practiced, it would have eliminated all these problems. These events clearly revealed that the Gospel of Jesus Christ must be spread abroad as effectively and as quickly as possible, because it alone carries the message of redemption to enable men of every race and nationality to have the strength and motivation from God to do what is right.

The second essential is *judgment*. This word is also fraught with meaning and alive with power for good. One meaning of this word is "the ability to come to a proper understanding of things." It is the power to compare and sort out right from wrong and then to make good and sound decisions. A man of sound judgment is a man who has good sense. This is critical in a world filled with complex problems in which each day seems to add others to the list.

The kind of leadership, that can tackle this maze of complicated and intricate difficulties and sort them out, untangle them, lay them out in a way to be understood, and then make good problem-solving decisions, is critically needed. The bitter hatreds, the pollution of the water and air, the depletion of our natural resources, the population explosion, the food shortages, the ability to provide aid following natural disasters such as earthquakes, floods, hurricanes, and typhoons—for these sound judgment is urgently needed.

The third word is *equity,* which speaks of fairness, impartiality, and justice. Today, millions of people are uptight because their employers, their employees, their professors, their husband or wives, their kings, presidents, or prime ministers have treated them unfairly. The decisions were not impartial and justice was not done. The results have been strikes or riots, divorce, and violence of every kind.

A world in which righteousness, judgment, and equity prevail is needed. And such a world can only come when men follow the teachings of the Word of God. At both the individual and corporate levels, then, men and women need to commit themselves to seeking after God through His Word. If they do that, *then* they will understand the fear of the Lord, find the knowledge of God, and understand righteousness, judgment, and equity. That indeed *is* the good path.

4

The Moral Safeguard of Wisdom

Proverbs 2:10—3:10

Unwholesome influences of the world crowd around us. The Christian is constantly being pressed to conform to it. The believer is pressured to lower his standards, to compromise a little here, to give up a little there, to join the crowd and be one of the boys or girls, and to quit being different. This is particularly tough on our young people, who feel these tensions and are under greater pressure, perhaps, than Christian adults.

The only preventive to succumbing to these deadly forces is to be in the Word of God and in prayer. The Book of Proverbs was written to warn those pursuing the paths of evil and to show the beleagered believers how to live in this evil-plagued world. Solomon has warned everyone that the ways of evil lead to destruction and has made a fervent appeal for men and women to follow wisdom (Prov. 1:8-33). He has also spelled out the means by which the simple one, the scorner, and the rebel can come back to God and join others in the pursuit of wisdom (2:1-5). Those who do this are promised the preserving care of Almighty God (2:6-9).

Solomon now turns to a discussion of the protective power of wisdom (2:10-22), noting *how* God will preserve His own and illustrating how wisdom will help us resist the temptations of evil men and women. He teaches that it takes a whole-

47

hearted commitment on the part of the believer to appropriate that protection from God (3:1-10). Wisdom becomes a moral safeguard for the disciple.

"When wisdom entereth into thine heart, and knowledge is pleasant unto thy soul, discretion shall preserve thee, [and] understanding shall keep thee" (2:10-11).

As already pointed out in the previous section (2:7-8 particularly), the wisdom of God has the power to preserve and protect those whose lives are governed by it. But the key to the whole process is that it must enter our hearts (2:10); this is a picture of a life subject to the will of God. When Jesus Christ is on the throne of our hearts, our lives are under His control. When we acknowledge His absolute lordship and commit ourselves to Him as His loyal disciples, then as our Lord and Master He will protect and preserve us who are His own.

When wisdom enters our hearts, it is like lemon juice and sugar being added to water. The color and the taste are changed as the liquid now becomes tangy and refreshing. It is diffused throughout the entire glass or pitcher, for it has taken over the entity of water through chemical change.

Solomon speaks of the person who gladly acknowledges a new master. He does not look on submission to the will of God as some form of bondage, but as the highest, best, and most pleasant experience of life. He echoes the words of the psalmist, "How sweet are Thy words unto my taste! Yea, sweeter than honey to my mouth!" (Ps. 119:103) The practice of obedience to God is not unpleasant work that has to be done, but an experience of joy and delight.

The worth of God's wisdom is beyond measure. It keeps us from the paths of sin which lead to total ruin This makes wisdom far more valuable than all the wealth of the world, "for what shall it profit a man, if he gain the whole world, and lose his own soul?" (Mark 8:36)

Having wisdom and knowledge in the heart and soul results in two things. First, wisdom guides us positively in the way of virtue and truth by teaching us discretion. That in itself is a remarkable thing in a world filled with sin and unrighteousness. Second, it arms us against the temptations and sins which beset us on every hand by giving us the understanding to avoid them.

The psalmist said, "Concerning the works of men, by the word of Thy lips I have kept me from the paths of the destroyer" (Ps. 17:4). Wisdom is an armor of defense against the fiery darts of the devil, the corruption of our own flesh, and the allurements of the world. Solomon also said that "wisdom is better than strength" and "wisdom is better than weapons of war" (Ecc. 9:16, 18).

In order to be effective, wisdom must sink deeply into our hearts and permeate our souls. If the wisdom of God is merely kept in mind as an interesting fact or curiosity, it will not inflame our hearts and spirits to follow God and to guide our wills in the paths of truth.

"To deliver thee from the way of the evil man, from the man that speaketh froward things; who leave the paths of uprightness, to walk in the ways of darkness; who rejoice to do evil, and delight in the frowardness of the wicked; whose ways are crooked, and they froward in their paths" (2:12-15).

If men and women could only see the ugly and wretched deformity of sin and where it ultimately leads, their hearts would recoil in horror and disgust. But sin never presents itself as it really is. It is like a sugarcoated capsule of cyanide. It is like a hypodermic needle that is said to contain an anticholera vaccine, but in reality is filled with the venom of a cobra. It is like a path which is marked as the way to joy and pleasure, but which actually leads to the miseries of hell; it is always crooked and hides the end from view. Once a person is on his way down the path that leads to destruction, only the powerful intervention of the grace of God can save him.

In this passage Solomon exposes the various traps of sin as a fearful picture of temptation and evil. It is fascinating to observe that the primary warning is against evil companions, for they are one of the major means of leading people—particularly youth—astray. If a young person would avoid the heartache and sorrow at the end of the trail, he must pick his friends and companions with care. Today's society swarms with hordes of men and women whose prime mission in life seems to be to ensnare others in their life-style of evil. For example, in the areas of drugs and sexual perversion, pushers and pimps abound in many schools and neighborhood hangouts.

Throngs of these evil-minded, hellbent sinners swagger through the streets of our cities doing their dead-level best to entice unsuspecting youth into a life of wanton immorality. Like poisoned fountains spewing forth death and destruction, their lips reveal what their hearts contain—a vituperative hatred for God, His ways, and His Word. Their contamination spreads like the foul stench of an open sewer; being polluted themselves, they pollute everyone around them. Like the devil himself, they gloat and glory in wickedness and strive to draw others into their net of abominable evils.

The promise of wisdom as a deliverance contrasts starkly with this picture of terrifying and ultimate doom. The promise of wisdom is to snatch us from the very jaws of death, to take us through life on the paths of uprightness and light, to lead us on the straight path of communion and fellowship with the eternal God, and to let us experience the joys of a truly abundant life.

Moses, in his last speech to the people of Israel, placed a choice before them. It is the same choice with which God confronts us today. "I call heaven and earth to record this day against you, that I have set before you life and death, blessing and cursing; therefore choose life, that both thou and thy seed may live; that thou mayest love the Lord thy God, and that thou mayest obey His voice, and that thou mayest cleave unto Him: for He is thy life, and the length of thy days" (Deut. 30:19-20).

The warning is clear; we must choose to go the way of wisdom.

"To deliver thee from the strange woman, even for the stranger which flattereth with her words; which forsaketh the guide of her youth, and forgetteth the covenant of her God. For her house inclineth unto death, and her paths unto the dead. None that go unto her return again, neither take they hold of the paths of life" (2:16-19).

This passage introduces us to the snare of the lust of the flesh and immorality. The strange woman is described as one who flatters with her tongue, who has forsaken the path of virtue and purity, and who has forgotten the Word and wisdom of God. She is called a stranger for two reasons. In Israel, all those who were outside the covenant fold of God, who followed the ways of Baal or other gods, who were trained in the ways and laws of the heathen, who worshiped strange gods and practiced the religion of the nations around them, were called strangers. As such, this woman was to be a stranger to the men of God if they were to remain faithful to the Lord.

God clearly predicted what would happen if His people intermingled and intermarried with the heathen. They would learn their pagan ways and would forsake the God of their fathers. The women of the nations around them were raised with a lax view of morality and would not consider themselves bound by the strict laws of purity and virtue that God required of His people. Their standards being different, their outlook was governed by corrupt practices, and their life-styles contained nothing of the truth of God.

The second reason she is called a stranger is that the Israelites were also to count as strangers the women of their own land who had forsaken the principles of holiness, purity, virtue, and honor. They were to be shunned as if they were heathen. Just as Samson was deluded by Delilah, so men are tricked by the flattery and deceit of a woman of low morals as she practices her wiles on their unsuspecting hearts. As the ox goes unsuspectingly to the slaughter, so the man who follows such a woman is led along the pathway of death.

This description is also characteristic of a woman who is unfaithful to her husband and to the vows she made before God. She has broken her promise to forsake all others and keep herself only for him. Most of all, she has broken her promise to God and He does not look lightly on broken vows. Solomon warned, "When thou vowest a vow unto God, defer not to pay it; for He hath no pleasure in fools; pay that which thou hast vowed. Better is it that thou shouldest not vow, than that thou shouldest vow and not pay. Suffer not thy mouth to cause thy flesh to sin; neither say thou before the angel, that it was an error; wherefore should God be angry at thy voice, and destroy the work of thine hands?" (Ecc. 5:4-6)

The sin of immorality is deadly. And it works in both directions—a man can entice a woman into sin as well, with Solomon's descriptions fitting him as a stranger also. This sin deadens the soul, dampens one's affections toward God, and incurs God's judgment.

Jesus Christ gave clear instructions that we are to be ruthless in dealing with immorality. "Ye have heard that it was said by them of old time, 'Thou shalt not commit adultery.' But I say unto you, that whosoever looketh on a woman to lust after her hath committed adultery with her already in his heart. And if thy right eye offend thee, pluck it out, and cast it from thee; for it is profitable for thee that one of thy members should perish, and not that thy whole body should be cast into hell" (Matt. 5:27-29).

Those who are caught up in this tangled web rarely recover. The heart becomes hardened and the mind blinded. People involved in this sin start to justify their actions and rationalize their behavior, as a minister in an eastern city did. For years he carried on an affair with another woman, and his wife suffered in silence. Finally, unable to take it any longer, she exposed him to the church board. The minister defended his actions, saying that it was just a weakness. Other people indulge in other fleshly pursuits—his just simply happened to be illicit sex. Only the wisdom of God can keep us from being captured by the evil of a carnal mind and the appetites of the flesh. The clear warning should ever be before us.

"That thou mayest walk in the way of good men, and keep the paths of the righteous. For the upright shall dwell in the land, and the perfect shall remain in it. But the wicked shall be cut off from the earth, and the transgressor shall be rooted out of it" (2:20-22).

Good men have always walked the same path. What was right yesterday is right today; what was true last year is true today. The wisdom of God will lead us directly into that which is good and right and true. In the preceding sections we saw how godly wisdom will protect and preserve us from evil; in these verses we are reminded again of the positive effect of wisdom on the soul.

Jeremiah reminded his generation, "Thus saith the Lord,

'Stand ye in the ways, and see, and ask for the old paths, where is the good way, and walk therein, and ye shall find rest for your souls' " (Jer. 6:16). It was the desire of the writer of Hebrews "that ye be not slothful, but followers of them who through faith and patience inherit the promises" (Heb. 6:12).

The instruction here is not only to walk in the right path, but to keep to the paths of the righteous. So often in our Christian growth, there comes an interlude with sin or a lapse into some of the old ways. Many have testified that after they became Christians they drifted back to some of the old sins for a while. Often there is the first flush of excitement at the time of conversion. Then it begins to fade and the allurements of the old life grow stronger and stronger. "Look what you're missing," some old friends might say.

Why does this happen? All too often the new Christian does not have some older believer to set the example for him. He has no one to whom he can turn, and who will take a personal interest in his spiritual welfare. Remember that the devil has an extremely effective follow-up program for young Christians. When he loses them from the kingdom of darkness, he tries to nullify their effectiveness in the kingdom of God. He causes the influences of evil men to be brought to bear on the new believer.

The greatest need of the young Christian is for some good and faithful saints to show him the way along the path of his new life. Often they can lead a straying young convert back to the path of righteousness. But how much better it is for an older Christian to provide the influence of a godly life right from the time that a believer responds to the call of the Gospel and is born again into the family of God. As a new babe in Christ he certainly needs someone to show him the way and to care for his soul. He needs to be guided in the ways of good men. Then he shall dwell in the land and remain in it, and not wander into the byways of sin and destruction. The psalmist stated, "The righteous shall inherit the land, and dwell therein forever. Wait on the Lord, and keep His way, and He shall exalt thee to inherit the land; when the wicked are cut off, thou shalt see it. Mark the perfect man, and behold the upright, for the end of that man is peace" (Ps. 37:29, 34, 37).

The contrast to this is quite clear: the wicked shall be cut off from the earth and rooted out of it. All this makes it abundantly clear that we must be diligent to fill our minds with the heavenly wisdom of God and be certain to cultivate a taste for His ways, His will, and His Word.

"My son, forget not My law; but let thine heart keep My commandments; for length of days, and long life, and peace, shall they add to thee. Let not mercy and truth forsake thee: bind them about thy neck; write them upon the table of thine heart: So shalt thou find favor and good understanding in the sight of God and man" (3:1-4).

As I look back on my early training as a Christian, I am especially grateful that the man who started me in Scripture memory stressed the need for review. We must not only memorize the Word of God, but we must do what we can to see that we don't forget it; and the secret of successful retentive memory is review, review, review.

My method was quite simple. Since I had to walk to work, I reviewed my verses on the way to and from work. I rode the streetcar to school, so I worked on them during that time as well. I had gone to a Navigator conference and had gotten confused as to what the system of review should be. Somehow I had gotten the idea that I should review each verse seven times a day. Later I discovered that we were to review each verse once a day for seven weeks after we had memorized it. But I had begun to review each verse seven times a day, and it took every spare minute of my time to do it. But I really learned some Scriptures.

The secret of review is consistency. Think of all the time you waste when you could be memorizing and reviewing the Word of God. One method is to put the verses on small cards so that they can be carried wherever you go. The Navigators *Topical Memory System* is printed on cards and is accompanied by instructions and a convenient pack in which to carry them.* I carried that pack of verses and worked on them all the time. Today there are thousands of men and women who are making

---

*The Topical Memory System is available for $5 from your local Christian bookstore or from NavPress, P.O. Box 20, Colorado Springs, Colorado 80901.

their time pay double by working on their Scripture memory and review as they do other things.

Homemakers can work on their verses while they wash the dishes or iron. Men can put their cards on the mirror and learn them while they shave. Drivers can place their packs on the seats of their cars and review them while waiting for a red light to change. Those who ride busses or trains can review while going from one place to another and waiting for their transportation. When people get home from work and have a few minutes to spare, they can get out their packs and go to work on their Scriptures.

Here is a challenge: for one week keep track of how much time you waste when you could be following the command of this passage, "Forget not My law, but let thine heart keep My commandments" (Prov. 3:1).

Notice well the blessing that follows: a long, full life filled with peace. The Word of God is a great source of inner strength and peace in troubled times. David stated, "The Lord will give strength unto His people; the Lord will bless His people with peace" (Ps. 29:11).

But it takes discipline, diligence, and commitment on our part to make it work. These are the essence of discipleship. God's warning and encouragement to a new generation is worthy of note: "Only take heed to thyself, and keep thy soul diligently, lest thou forget the things which thine eyes have seen, and lest they depart from thy heart all the days of thy life: but teach them thy sons, and thy sons' sons" (Deut. 4:9).

Solomon follows the promise of blessing with a strong challenge. As you study the Scriptures you discover that the mercy of God and the truth of God are inseparably linked together. These two words are often joined together in a beautiful harmony of blessing and love. Jacob saw them as the gifts of God of which he was not worthy, "I am not worthy of the least of all the mercies, and of all the truth, which Thou hast showed unto Thy servant" (Gen. 32:10). The psalmist saw them as the object of everlasting thanksgiving, "Enter into His gates with thanksgiving, and into His courts with praise: be thankful unto Him, and bless His name. For the Lord is good; His mercy is everlasting; and His truth endureth to all generations" (Ps. 100:4-5).

The mercy and truth of God were to be the cause of praise from all the people of all lands. "O praise the Lord, all ye nations: praise Him, all ye people. For His merciful kindness is great toward us, and the truth of the Lord endureth forever. Praise ye the Lord" (Ps. 117:1-2). In Scripture these two graces often go hand in hand.

Now if that is true of the character of God, then it should be true of our lives as well. We are to bear a family resemblance to the Father and to His Son Jesus Christ. "Be ye therefore followers of God, as dear children; and walk in love, as Christ also hath loved us, and hath given Himself for us an offering and a sacrifice to God for a sweet-smelling savor" (Eph. 5:1-2).

But how often are these two attitudes of God missing from our daily experience? Mercy is becoming a stranger in the earth. Truth is hard to come by. As Christians we should make it a matter of daily prayer that God would enable us to salt the earth with mercy and truth as we go about the daily affairs of life.

Have you ever met people who are students of the Bible, who firmly profess its doctrinal truths, but are cantankerous and hard to get along with? They will fight for the truth of God at the drop of a hat, but their spirits toward others are as hard as flint. This is one of the reasons, perhaps, why God has placed mercy and truth together in His Word.

On the other hand there are people whose hearts are filled with concern, love, and mercy for others, but who have no compass point to direct them to the truth or who have no solid foundation. They are warm, generous, loving people who speak of believing whatever you want, that one set of beliefs is as good as the next. Sincerity is the key and tolerance is the hallmark of their faith.

The problem with that, of course, is that a person may be sincerely wrong. If you go to the medicine cabinet at night and take poison instead of cough syrup, it doesn't matter how sincere you were. You will still be dead wrong. So mercy, the spirit of love and gentleness, and truth must go together in our lives even as they shine forth as jewels in the character of God Himself.

The resulting promise is clear. The one who has these

godly traits as visible twin features in his personality and practice will find favor with both God and men. The blessings of God will shower down on him, even as the warm hand of friendship will be extended from his fellowmen. This was the testimony that Samuel bore, "The child Samuel grew on, and was in favor both with the Lord, and also with men" (1 Sam. 2:26). The greatest example of all is that of the Lord Jesus: "Jesus increased in wisdom and stature, and in favor with God and man" (Luke 2:52).

"Trust in the Lord with all thine heart, and lean not unto thine own understanding. In all thy ways acknowledge Him, and He shall direct thy paths" (3:5-6).

When God calls us to exercise faith in Him, it is to be a total and undivided commitment. Our hope, our confidence must be in God alone. No confidence in the flesh; no dependence on human wisdom. Naturally we resist that idea, in our pride and self-reliance. We want to lean on ourselves, to trust our own foolish and false ideas.

The Prophet Jeremiah has a word for us at this point: "Thus saith the Lord, 'Cursed be the man that trusteth in man, and maketh flesh his arm, and whose heart departeth from the Lord. For he shall be like the heath in the desert, and shall not see when good cometh; but shall inhabit the parched places in the wilderness, in a salt land and not inhabited'" (Jer. 17:5-6).

This is the story of Adam and Eve, and the history of mankind since the Fall. We want to go our own way and do our own thing, to lean on our own understanding. But our own understanding is likely to take us down the wrong path, in the wrong direction.

Paul explains it clearly. "This I say therefore, and testify in the Lord, that ye henceforth walk not as other Gentiles walk, in the vanity of their mind, having the understanding darkened, being alienated from the life of God through the ignorance that is in them, because of the blindness of their heart" (Eph. 4:17-18). He told the Romans, "Because that, when they knew God, they glorified Him not as God, neither were thankful; but became vain in their imaginations, and their foolish heart was darkened. Professing themselves to be wise, they became fools" (Rom. 1:21-22).

So the human mind by itself, without the illumination of the Holy Spirit, having been corrupted by the Fall, is a false and untrustworthy guide. Does this mean we are not to use our minds? Not at all. Dawson Trotman, founder of The Navigators, used to tell us, "God gave you an awful lot of leading when He gave you your mind." So faith in God strengthens, enlightens, and invigorates our minds.

Self-dependence is folly and rebellion is ruin. But to trust in the Lord is a dynamic, adventuresome, exciting life-style. Placing our faith totally in the power, goodness, and wisdom of God is the most sensible thing we can do or are ever likely to do.

The next step is to take all the ordinary matters of life to Him in prayer. To give lip service to God and then try and make do by ourselves is idolatry. Morning prayer, the practice of taking things to God before we have consulted human counselors or before we let things take their course, is important. This is a power that is much overlooked. David knew its worth, and so pledged, "My voice shalt Thou hear in the morning, O Lord; in the morning will I direct my prayer unto Thee, and will look up" (Ps. 5:3).

Stick with the Word and prayer. Don't go looking for new and strange revelations, the latest fad. Open your Bible and go through it with sober, practical, and reverent faith. God will never lead you astray, but "He shall direct thy paths." No step you take that you have prayed over will bring ultimate regret, for God will see you through.

A couple I know had Proverbs 3:5-6 engraved in their wedding bands. It is a commitment they made to God on their wedding day, and He has directed their paths through the struggles, adjustments, pains, and joys of their married life. It is this kind of commitment that God wants to see in each of His children, and it is based on a dedication to the Word and to prayer.

"Be not wise in thine own eyes; fear the Lord, and depart from evil. It shall be health to thy navel, and marrow to thy bones" (3:7-8).

Self-confidence is a mysterious thing. Held in the right way it can be a blessing, but held in the wrong way it can be a curse. The farmer, because of his background and training, is confident that he knows how to plant corn, raise cattle, and harvest the crops. The carpenter, because of his background and training, is confident that he can put in a window, hang a door, or fix the roof. The doctor, because of his background and training, knows he can set a bone, treat a rash, or settle a queasy stomach. That's the right kind of confidence and without it the corn would not get planted, the door would not get hung, and the broken bone would not get set.

But there is another form of self-confidence that leads to pride and stifles growth. It is true that many men and women could attain great heights in their professions if they were eager to be taught. But all too often many feel that they already know it all. So they hit a plateau, go no farther in their profession, and their self-confidence becomes a curse.

Many could become wise if they didn't think they had already arrived. Since they are wise in their own eyes, they are not eager to learn to respond to the suggestions of others. In fact, all too often a suggestion given in love and the right spirit is refused because the person feels he is being put down or degraded.

Some feel that to accept something from another is a sign of weakness or an admission of stupidity. "Who is a wise man and endued with knowledge among you? Let him show out of a good conversation his works with meekness of wisdom. But if ye have bitter envying and strife in your hearts, glory not, and lie not against the truth. This wisdom descendeth not from above, but is earthly, sensual, devilish. For where envying and strife is, there is confusion and every evil work" (James 3:13-16).

The Apostle Paul instructed the Romans, "For I say, through the grace given unto me, to every man that is among you, not to think of himself more highly than he ought to think; but to think soberly, according as God hath dealt to every man the measure of faith. . . . Be of the same mind one toward another. Mind not high things, but condescend to men of low estate. Be not wise in your own conceits" (Rom. 12:3, 16). The Prophet Isaiah pronounced a woe on this very thing:

"Woe unto them that are wise in their own eyes, and prudent in their own sight!" (Isa. 5:21)

The next admonition is to fear the Lord and depart from sin. These two things go together. When Joseph was tempted to sin, he refused and asked, "How can I do this great wickedness, and sin against God?" (Gen. 39:9) When Nehemiah was recounting his record as governor, he recalled how others before him had overcharged and cheated the people. "But," he said, "so did not I, because of the fear of God" (Neh. 5:15). Job had come to the same conclusion, "And unto man He said, 'Behold, the fear of the Lord, that is wisdom; and to depart from evil is understanding'" (Job 28:28). One of the things the cross of Jesus Christ portrays is the love of God. His love for you is so deep and abiding that His only begotten Son died for you. It is also a clear picture of the hatred God has for sin. He was willing to go to the limit, even the death of His Son, to free you from the condemnation and power of sin.

This means we must take the admonition of this passage seriously. We cannot toy with sin and still claim to love and reverence God. The two are mutually exclusive; they cannot live together in the same life. A wonderful promise comes with obedience to this command—the promise of health to body and soul. Today medical science is telling us that many of our diseases can be traced back to a nagging conscience, worry over deeds done in the past, and a fretful spirit. Likewise, our souls will prosper and be in good health when we maintain communion with God and turn from the paths and hidden pitfalls of sin.

For those who have forsaken the ways of God but desire to return to Him, God promises, "I will heal their backsliding, I will love them freely, for Mine anger is turned away from him" (Hosea 14:4). The Prophet Malachi also records a similar promise, "Unto you that fear My name shall the Sun of righteousness arise with healing in His wings; and ye shall go forth, and grow up as calves of the stall" (Mal. 4:2).

"Honor the Lord with thy substance, and with the firstfruits of all thine increase: so shall thy barns be filled with plenty, and thy presses shall burst out with new wine" (3:9-10).

During a summer conference I was directing at Glen Eyrie, the Navigators' conference center in Colorado Springs, staff member Rod Sargent spoke on the subject of giving. Before he began his message, he took a poll of his audience. The question was this: "Do you feel you are a generous person?" He asked the 200 or so conferees to answer with a simple yes or no. When he had gathered and tabulated the responses, the overwhelming majority had answered "no" on their slips of paper. In fact, all but about half a dozen had answered negatively. Yet these people were all Christians, most of them carrying important responsibilities in their local churches.

The conclusion of Solomon's exhortation to total commitment ends with a call to generous giving. The two verses give a command and a promise. We are told to honor the Lord with our lives. The way we live, think, and act are all to honor Him. This passage further teaches that we are to honor Him with our substance.

What does that mean? It means that we use what we have in a way that honors God. It is much more than just merely giving money for His work. Do we use our cars to honor the Lord? Do we use our bank accounts to honor Him? How about our golf clubs, tennis racquets, TV sets? The command is clear: "Honor the Lord with thy substance."

Then Solomon goes on to say, "With the firstfruits of all thine increase." When riches increase, we are tempted to honor ourselves and set our hearts on the things of this world. Three words stand out in this statement: (1) firstfruits—God who is first and best should have the first and best; (2) all—in everything with which God has prospered us, we should honor Him; and (3) thine—it is yours, for God gave it to you to be used according to His will and Word. It is not how much you have, but what you do with what you have; how you use it.

Then comes the promise. Jesus gave a similar promise during His ministry, "Give, and it shall be given unto you; good measure, pressed down, and shaken together, and running over, shall men give into your bosom. For with the same measure that ye mete withal it shall be measured to you again" (Luke 6:38).

So part of the response of discipleship is the giving of our substance to honor the Lord. And this can only be done as we have committed ourselves to the Word and to prayer. For that is the way of wisdom, and that is the way we avoid evil. We let wisdom enter our hearts (Prov. 2:10), which enables us to keep God's commandments (3:1). The result of that is His directing us in all our paths.

5

The Reward of Finding Wisdom

Proverbs 3:11-26

The results of a statistical analysis once declared that in the history of the human race there has never been a child that was reared properly. In raising kids you look at your record and must admit that you've made some mistakes. All of us have. We've all blown it one way or another. We have prayed and done what we thought was right. We did the best we could in the sight of God and have trusted Him to put it all together and add His blessing to our attempts.

God, on the other hand, is the perfect Father. He has never made a mistake—not one! Think of all the children born into His family over the centuries, and He reared everyone in exactly the right way. He has never had to look back and say, "I shouldn't have done that" or, "If I had to do it over, I would have done it another way."

"My son, despise not the chastening of the Lord; neither be weary of His correction: for whom the Lord loveth He correcteth; even as a father the son in whom he delighteth" (3:11-12).

From time to time God's children need correction and discipline. Now if we're like most human beings, we do not care

63

to be corrected or disciplined. But for the Christian the blessing is that God knows exactly what we need and how to apply it to our lives to teach us the lessons He wants us to learn. His timing is always perfect. As the prophet said, "Therefore will the Lord wait, that He may be gracious unto you, and therefore will He be exalted, that He may have mercy upon you: for the Lord is a God of judgment: blessed are all they that wait for Him" (Isa. 30:18). That is why Peter said, "Humble yourselves therefore under the mighty hand of God, that He may exalt you in due time" (1 Peter 5:6).

This wisdom gained through discipline, as spoken of in Proverbs, is not the innate ability of men to wisely conduct their affairs in this world. It is not something that the geniuses throughout history possessed naturally. Solomon's presentation of wisdom has two important characteristics. First, it is *religious* and is based on the fear of the Lord, the proper reverence men are to have for God. Second, it is *practical* and must be seen in proper human conduct. It is knowledge of God's truth through His Word, and the application of it to life.

To seek after wisdom demands a commitment—we dedicate ourselves wholeheartedly to taking in the Word of God individually and personally and to crying unto Him through prayer. We then trust in the Lord totally to direct our paths through life. In this section we see that wisdom, though it sometimes requires this kind of fatherly discipline to appropriate, brings with it great blessings.

God always uses the most sure and loving means to accomplish His objectives in our lives. "The Lord will not cast off forever: but though He cause grief, yet will He have compassion according to the multitude of His mercies. For He doth not afflict willingly nor grieve the children of men" (Lam. 3:31-33). When you consider the enormity of our sins, it is a marvel that God's fatherly correction is so gentle and light. When Ezra prayed his great confession, that fact was foremost in his mind. "And after all that is come upon us for our evil deeds, and for our great trespass, seeing that Thou our God has punished us less than our iniquities deserve, and hast given us such deliverance as this" (Ezra 9:13).

David glorified in this wonderful truth, "He hath not dealt

with us after our sins; nor rewarded us according to our iniquities. For as the heaven is high above the earth, so great is His mercy toward them that fear Him. As far as east is from the west, so far hath He removed our transgressions from us. Like as a father pitieth his children, so the Lord pitieth them that fear Him. For He knoweth our frame; He remembereth that we are dust" (Ps. 103:10-14). Jeremiah reminded the people that the chastisement of God was just, "Wherefore doth a living man complain, a man for the punishment of his sins?" (Lam. 3:39)

But in the dark season of correction, it is easy to forget that blessed truth. We are prone to complain. We feel that the affliction is harder or lasts longer than it should. Often we feel that deliverance will never come simply because it does not arrive when we feel it should. However, it is foolish to complain and contend with God in light of His sovereignty and power.

It is the height of folly to think that God would bring anything to bear in our lives that was not for our very best. His correction never comes as that of a judge dispensing punishment; it comes as from a father who only wants to bring his children back to the safe path and a secure fellowship with himself. He corrects us because He loves us.

God's glorious aim must always be kept in view. He is doing whatever is necessary to conform us more and more into the image of His Son, the Lord Jesus Christ. The writer to the Hebrews gives us an amazing insight into the earthly life of the Saviour, "Though He were a Son, yet learned He obedience by the things which He suffered" (Heb. 5:8). We can learn the same great lessons as we respond in loving surrender to the will of God.

"Happy is the man that findeth wisdom, and the man that getteth understanding. For the merchandise of it is better than the merchandise of silver, and the gain thereof than fine gold. She is more precious than rubies: and all the things thou canst desire are not to be compared unto her" (3:13-15).

The hope of gaining something good is incentive to work hard. On one of my days of working out at the gym I saw an elderly man who was sweating and straining as he pushed and pulled the various weights and exercise equipment. His incentive was better health and a longer life. Across the room was a young muscle builder. He too was sweating and straining, but he probably didn't have health and a longer life in mind. Likely he wanted muscles that would bulge under his shirt as he strutted down Main Street.

This passage begins with a promise of finding something good; the man who finds wisdom finds happiness. In other sections we have found other fruits of wisdom, but here we find the happy man who has discovered something worth more than gold, silver, or precious rubies. It is evident that Solomon is not talking here about the wisdom of the world. Those who have searched for it, found it, and tested it have found it lacking. It does not bring the happiness spoken of here. Other Scriptures confirm this.

"I communed with mine own heart, saying, 'Lo, I am come to great estate, and have gotten more wisdom than all they that have been before me in Jerusalem; yea, my heart had great experience of wisdom and knowledge.' And I gave my heart to know wisdom, and to know madness and folly; I perceived that this also is vexation of spirit. For in much wisdom is much grief; and he that increaseth knowledge increaseth sorrow" (Ecc. 1:16-18).

It is obvious, then, that in this passage from Proverbs 3, Solomon is speaking of the wisdom of God. The Apostle Paul communicated the same excitement and joy when he discovered Jesus. "But what things were gain to me, those I counted loss for Christ. Yea, doubtless, and I count all things but loss for the excellency of the knowledge of Christ Jesus my Lord: for whom I have suffered the loss of all things, and do count them but dung, that I may win Christ" (Phil. 3:7-8). His power, prestige, position, and all the things he gloried in, were now so much refuse in comparison with the knowledge of Jesus Christ. Paul had found the true source of joy, even in the midst of trial and tribulation. "But none of these things move me, neither count I my life dear unto myself, so that I might finish my course with joy, and the ministry, which I have received of the Lord Jesus, to testify the Gospel of the grace of God" (Acts 20:24).

This passage also speaks of the merchandise of wisdom, which at first glance is a rather unusual phrase. But when you think about it, a beautiful truth comes to the surface. The gaining of the wisdom of God must be our prime endeavor in life, and not just a by-product. The good businessman keeps his thoughts and attention directed to the selling of his goods in order that his business might prosper. His livelihood and the welfare of his family and employees depend on his careful attention to business.

Jesus also spoke of the merchant who had discovered a thing of great value and ventured his all to gain it. "The kingdom of heaven is like unto a merchant man, seeking goodly pearls, who, when he had found one pearl of great price, went and sold all that he had, and bought it" (Matt. 13:45-46).

Transcendent happiness fills the heart of the one who enjoys fellowship with Jesus Christ and is daily enjoying the spiritual blessings freely given from the hand of his heavenly Father. The person who has discovered the richness of God's grace knows it is far more valuable than the wealth of this world and that it is the kind of treasure the wealth of the world can't buy. It is something the world cannot give because it knows nothing about it. Nothing can be compared to the joy and happiness that comes from living close to the Lord and being taught by the wisdom of heaven.

"Length of days is in her right hand; and in her left hand riches and honor. Her ways are ways of pleasantness, and all her paths are peace. She is a tree of life to them that lay hold upon her: and happy is everyone that retaineth her" (3:16-18).

Pleasure is an elusive thing. All too often those who live for it never find it. Those who go out to have a good time frequently return disappointed. If pleasure is the objective, it is rarely achieved. In this passage we learn of the paths to happiness, pleasantness, and peace. Wisdom's ways are not only maligned by the world, but are often hidden from it.

A group of high school kids decided to do something for the shut-ins of their church. So they put together some baskets of fresh fruit, split up in teams of three and four, and launched out. They spent a whole evening chatting with the elderly.

They found errands to run and beds to make. But most of all they found lonely hearts to cheer.

They looked at old dog-eared scrapbooks and picture albums of a time that was past. They talked and laughed and learned much. Finally, when they regrouped at the church for a late evening snack, their spirits were higher than kites in March. They had known the evening would be worthwhile, but they had never suspected it would be so much fun. They had not only done something that was good and decent, but they had done something that was really enjoyable to them. They had gained some valuable insights into the wisdom of God.

One of the ministers of our church once took his Sunday School class to a Christian camp. As they spent the day on the grounds, he was struck by the life-style of those who worked at that camp. Their only objective seemed to be to discover ways of serving those who came there. And they were happy. Truly happy. What they did for others did not emerge out of a set of rules and regulations which said, "You are here to serve, so get busy and serve!" Such a life-style grew out of some deep convictions that had been acquired over the years to make them want to serve others willingly.

So the way to a pleasant life, true happiness, and joy is to get out of ourselves and into the lives of others. This is the wisdom of God—true servanthood—to get our minds and attention on others and off ourselves. Length of days, true riches and honor, pleasantness and peace, fruits of the abundant life, and happiness are in the hands of wisdom being dispensed to anyone who will receive them.

In contrast, the world has never really discovered this and is on its mad scramble for these things, heading down the wrong path in the wrong direction. Self is at the center of men's search. And they work themselves into a frenzy, spending their time and money looking in the wrong places. But the wisdom of God is there for anyone who will hearken and receive it on God's terms.

"The Lord by wisdom hath founded the earth; by understanding hath He established the heavens. By His knowledge the depths are broken up, and the clouds drop down the dew" (3:19-20).

We have looked at the wisdom of God and its effects on the lives of the people of God. We have seen its fruits in the lives of those who will apply its teachings and follow its ways. Now we turn our attention to its effects on the world around us. This passage focuses our thoughts on the beginning, the creation of the world. The psalmist said, "O Lord, how manifold are Thy works! In wisdom hast Thou made them all; the earth is full of Thy riches" (Ps. 104:24).

We look at the creation of God, the world around us, and we are awed by its mysteries, thunderous power, delicate balance, beauty, and the marvel of the wisdom behind it all. We are overwhelmed by its amazing complexity meshed into a pattern of changeless laws. When we consider the heavens and the work of the hands of God, we can only say with David, "O Lord, our Lord, how excellent is Thy name in all the earth" (Ps. 8:9).

The Prophet Jeremiah declared, "He hath made the earth by His power, He hath established the world by His wisdom, and hath stretched out the heavens by His discretion. When He uttereth His voice, there is a multitude of waters in the heavens, and He causeth the vapors to ascend from the ends of the earth; He maketh lightnings with rain, and bringeth forth the wind out of His treasures" (Jer. 10:12-13).

We marvel at the wisdom of God as He broke up the depths and fashioned the rushing rivers and quiet streams. We watch in wonder as the clouds of the heavens collect the moisture and release it on the parched and thirsty ground. The planets and the stars speed through limitless space, the birds of the air soar through the sky, and all in perfect harmony and order. The seasons come and go, crops are planted and harvested— all through the work of God.

We look at it all and see the goodness and wisdom of God. The universe glitters with the infinite beauty and grandeur of the Almighty. "The heavens declare the glory of God; and the firmament showeth His handiwork" (Ps. 19:1).

A question comes to us as we consider the works of God. We can see *what* God has done by looking around us. We even know *how* it was done—He created all things by the Word of His power. He spoke all things into being. But *why?*

The Word of God gives a number of reasons, but one is

quite meaningful and personal to each of us in our daily walk with the Lord. He has created it all for our good and for our enjoyment. The Great Shepherd leads His people to the still waters and green fields of His pasture and encourages us to enjoy what He has provided to refresh our bodies and restore our souls.

Note that God the Father, God the Son, and God the Holy Spirit acted together at the creation of the world. The Bible says that the Spirit of God moved on the face of the waters (Gen. 1:2). And Paul states that through the Son of God "were all things created, that are in heaven, and that are in earth, visible and invisible, whether they be thrones, or dominions, or principalities, or powers: all things were created by Him and for Him" (Col. 1:16).

When you look at the physical universe around you, it should remind you of Jesus Christ, for all things were created by Him and for Him—all things physical and spiritual. He is also the Author of our faith, for He alone can give eternal life to those who come to God by Him. By the power of the creative Word of God physical and spiritual life began. "Being born again, not of corruptible seed, but of incorruptible, by the Word of God, which liveth and abideth forever" (1 Peter 1:23).

"My son, let not them depart from thine eyes: keep sound wisdom and discretion: so shall they be life unto thy soul, and grace to thy neck" (3:21-22).

As we study the Book of Proverbs, some things seem to be repeated many times. Are these vain repetitions of the same old things, said in a different way, perhaps, but nevertheless with nothing new to commend them? Hardly. Every Word of God is pure. Some things, however, are repeated from time to time for emphasis and to help insure our not missing them.

Teaching the truth of God can be a difficult matter. Our minds are dull; we rarely pick up something the first time around, especially spiritual truth.

The Lord's objective is to implant the wisdom of God in our hearts, but He works at it patiently. Rarely do we learn the lesson the first time. God sends His truth to us by the

Holy Spirit, but we cannot quite grasp it. So He sends it again from another angle. This time it strikes a little closer, but we're still unable to take it in. He finally breaks through to us, and we see what it is all about. In this book, the Lord is doing that with us through Solomon. He reveals one facet of a thing, lets it soak in for awhile, and then shows it to us from another angle.

In this passage we get another look at the wisdom of God. We are told to hold it fast and keep it secure. Held as a passing idea, it will do us little good. But if it becomes the guiding principle of life, it will stand us in good stead for eternity.

The first result of our keeping it secure is that it will be "life to thy soul." The wisdom of the world is totally devoid of life and energy. The unregenerate soul is alienated from the life of God and is therefore dead. But the psalmist records a tremendous promise from God, "Thy testimonies are wonderful, therefore doth my soul keep them. The entrance of Thy words giveth light; it giveth understanding unto the simple" (Ps. 119:129-130). Solomon also said, "Wisdom is a defence, and money is a defence; but the excellency of knowledge is, that wisdom giveth life to them that have it" (Ecc. 7:12).

The wisdom of God is also an ornament of grace to the life that is governed by it. That life is attractive. It shines with the inner luster of sound judgment and discretion. People like that glow with a quiet confidence that comes from living under the shadow of the Almighty. They have walked with Him, learned from Him, and obeyed Him. You can see it in their eyes, hear it in their speech, and observe it in their lives. Their souls are alive; their countenances are made bright by the inner glow of the power of God actively at work within them.

This is the promise to the one who walks steadfastly along wisdom's path: "The Lord taketh pleasure in His people; He will beautify the meek with salvation" (Ps. 149:4).

"Then shalt thou walk in thy way safely, and thy foot shall not stumble. When thou liest down, thou shalt not be afraid: yea, thou shalt lie down, and thy sleep shall be sweet. Be not afraid of sudden fear, neither of the desolation of the wicked, when it cometh. For the Lord shall be thy confidence, and shall keep thy foot from being taken" (3:23-26).

Most people have, at one time or another, walked along a dangerous path. One time in central Asia a friend and I were walking along a jungle path. A poisonous snake was hiding in a small thicket beside the path. When I saw it, I left the trail, jumped over a small stream, and got out of there as quickly as possible. I'm not sure I was in any real danger, but I didn't want to take any chances.

On another occasion I was on a high railroad bridge where one false step could have plunged me hundreds of feet to the ice of the frozen river below. The psalmist speaks of a time when he was not attentive to wisdom's words, "As for me, my feet were almost gone; my steps had well nigh slipped" (Ps. 73:2).

We have a double blessing in that God not only guides our waking times, but our hours of sleep as well. During times of turmoil and danger, nighttime can bring fear and distress. Men who have fought in war can testify to the dangers of the night. This passage speaks to that, for God promises that we can lie down and not be afraid, going to sleep and getting the needed rest.

For years my wife, Virginia, was afraid to be in the house alone at night. At one time we were living in a large, old three-story house that rattled and creaked in the wind. At night these strange noises would magnify greatly. She spent many a fitful and fearful hour listening to dangers that weren't really there. Then one day in her quiet time the Lord spoke to her from a verse that she knew was from the heart of God: "I will both lay me down in peace, and sleep; for Thou, Lord, only makest me dwell in safety" (Ps. 4:8). The problem has never recurred.

During World War II our ships were often in danger from two sources. The attacks of the enemy came from other ships and planes as they maneuvered for the great sea battles in the Pacific. We could see them coming and would brace ourselves for the shells and bombs that would soon be hurled at us. The other source of danger was a sneak attack by enemy submarines. Out of nowhere, when we least expected it, the torpedo could strike our ship. In this passage the Lord promises to be our confidence and convoy in time of trouble. He will see us safely through the dangerous and murky waters of sin and temptation. Peace and safety are the heritage of the child of God.

John Rogers was one of the martyrs during one of the great persecutions of the Christian Church. On the morning of his execution his tormentors found him fast asleep. Only with much shaking could he be roused out of his peaceful slumber. His sleep was sweet, for God was his confidence. "Thou wilt keep him in perfect peace, whose mind is stayed on Thee: because he trusteth in Thee. Trust ye in the Lord forever: for in the Lord Jehovah is everlasting strength. . . . 'Come, My people, enter thou into thy chambers, and shut thy doors about thee; hide thyself as it were for a little moment, until the indignation be overpast' " (Isa. 26:3-4, 20).

It is hard to believe that Almighty God has undertaken to protect each of His children but it is true. During our sojourn on this planet, we are under God's constant guidance and care. He has declared Himself to be our protector, our shield, our tower of defense. During times when our feet are on a slippery path—at night or during times of danger or distress— He is there to watch over us. He holds our hands, shows us the way, and protects us as we follow Him.

The parallel that Solomon has brought out in this section is that seeking wisdom means walking with God. And the rewards of doing so are tremendous—happiness in its fullest meaning, length of days, spiritual riches and honor, pleasantness, peace, abundant life, a good testimony, safety, a good night's sleep, and confidence. What more could a person ask for to have a satisfying life? These are things the world cannot give, but they are available to the man or woman who wants to walk with God.

6

Wisdom's Enemies and Inheritance

Proverbs 3:27-35

The person who walks in close fellowship with God, who acknowledges the Lord in all his ways (3:6), and who has his confidence in the Almighty (3:26) is the one who will obey Him in all things. That is discipleship, and in the Old Testament it is seen in the one who follows the positive admonitions in the Book of Proverbs, the one called the wise man in this marvelous book.

Proverbs 3 closes with some specific examples of what is expected of the wise man. Solomon lists behavior patterns that should characterize the seeker after divine wisdom. These are some things that he will do in his daily life, and other things that he will avoid doing because they are displeasing to the Lord.

This closing passage also continues the contrast between those who follow the Lord's ways and those who do not. Blessing, grace, and glory belong to the wise; cursing, scorn, and shame are the lot of fools.

"Withhold not good from them to whom it is due, when it is in the power of thine hand to do it. Say not unto thy neighbor, 'Go, and come again, and tomorrow I will give'; when thou hast it by thee" (3:27-28).

74

This is one of those passages having a wide variety of applications to the life of the child of God. The teaching is plain, straightforward, and easily understood: we should help others when we can.

I had been a Christian for about five years when I had my first encounter with this passage. I had memorized it a few weeks earlier, and it was fresh on my mind. I was relaxing with a group of seminary students on a Saturday afternoon discussing the weather, the baseball game, and other trivia. One of the men then said he thought he would go and wash his car. Since I was doing nothing, it was certainly in the power of my hand to help. So I got up and went out to the lot to wash the car with him. The rest of the group just sat there.

After we had washed the car, I was talking to one of the other men and he mentioned how nice it was of me to help in washing the car. So I showed him this passage and told him that the Lord had prompted me to do so by reminding me of the teaching contained in it.

He was dumbfounded. Apparently it had never entered his mind that the Bible gives practical guidance on everyday issues. To him it was a Book on which to base theological discussions and to do doctrinal research. The fact that God had used it to lead me to help another person wash his car completely blew his mind.

Jesus once told of a man who was mugged and robbed, and the religious leaders of the day just let him lie there in the sun half dead. Finally a man came along who had compassion on him, bound up his wounds, brought him to a hotel where he could recuperate, and even paid the bill. It was in the power of his hand to help and he did so. Jesus commended this Samaritan, and then told His listeners, "Go, and do thou likewise" (Luke 10:37; see 10:29-36). This well-known parable portrays a situation where a man felt compelled to put out some time, energy, and money to help someone in need. He got involved with his fellowman.

These opportunities come on us in many ways. One night my wife and I were waiting in a parking lot for another couple to join us. We were sitting in our car watching the traffic go by on a very busy street. Next to our lot a man was trying to leave his garage, but he couldn't find a break in the traffic. He just sat there and no one would let him in. Hundreds of drivers flashed by, saw him sitting there, but would not slow down. It would have cost them all of 10 seconds, but no one was willing to help him. Even though it was in the power of their hands to do it, they would not. Their neighbor was in need, but they just passed by.

Obviously, compassion and love form the basis of a life lived by these guidelines, and those things do not come easy. In fact, they rarely come at all without the empowering help of the Spirit of God. It is the way of God to anticipate the need and then make provision for it. His timing is always perfect and His provision is always abundant. What a blessing we would be to the world if we would cultivate that Christlike spirit.

"Devise not evil against thy neighbor, seeing he dwelleth securely by thee. Strive not with a man without cause, if he have done thee no harm. Envy thou not the oppressor, and choose none of his ways. For the froward is abomination to the Lord, but His secret is with the righteous" (3:29-32).

In the preceding passages we were instructed to do good. In these we are commanded *not* to do evil. Both admonitions are necessary for the balanced Christian life. Sometimes it is easier to avoid doing evil to my neighbor than it is to step out and do something positive for his good.

Take the matter of giving to missions to send the Gospel to the ends of the earth. What prevents many people from giving generously? Do they *hate* those who live in the non-Christian areas of the earth? Probably not. They don't *hate* heathen, but they *love* money. Somehow many of us have gotten our affections all tied up in things around us, and we know what our money can do to secure those things for us. So the mission program lags while we stuff our homes, closets, and garages full of the very latest fashions, fads, and gadgets.

In effect, what we do is disable ourselves by our extravagances. The open hand extended to the world, ready to heal and give, has tremendous power for good, but the clenched fist is the symbol for power, ready to grasp, control, and strike out in violence.

Then comes the injunction, "Devise not evil against thy neighbor." On a hill above our neighborhood some rather wealthy families live in large and ornate homes. A man decided to build his home among them, and for some reason one of the homeowners objected. The man went ahead anyway and built a very expensive home close to where the man with the objections lived. Soon bitterness arose between them, and they began to do malicious things to each other. Their evil deeds escalated to the point where one of the men killed the other's pet. Then came lawsuits, charges, and counter charges. These two men have been devising evil against one another ever since.

An old Chinese proverb states:
"Where there is peace in the heart, there is peace in the home.
Where there is peace in the home, there is peace in the neighborhood.
Where there is peace in the neighborhood, there is peace in the city.
Where there is peace in the city, there is peace in the land.
Where there is peace in the land, there is peace in the world."

James puts his finger right on the problem so many men face: "From whence come wars and fightings among you? Come they not hence, even of your lusts that war in your members? Ye lust, and have not: ye kill, and desire to have, and cannot obtain: ye fight and war, yet ye have not, because ye ask not" (James 4:1-2). It all begins in the heart, and as Bishop Fulton J. Sheen has said, "Jesus Christ is the One who came into the world to change the world by changing the human heart." Peace will never come into this world until the Prince of peace reigns in His splendor.

The love of power is universal. Men would rather rule than be ruled. They would rather be bosses telling others what to do than have to be told or "pushed around" by others. When a man comes home to report on his promotion and raise in pay, part of the thrill is that he now has more people reporting to him, and as a result has more power.

We admire power in sports. Even in the dignified and cultured sport of tennis, we read that "he really overpowered his opponent." Thousands of fans at a baseball game scream with exhilaration when their team crushes the opposition.

Men even stand in awe of machines that are big and powerful. During my first flight on the Boeing 747 Jumbo Jet, the chief steward announced over the intercom that we were flying on a marvelous airplane. He told us what it cost, how big it was, how many people it carried, and then told us of the power of the engines as compared to other jets. I recall the gasp of wonder that came from the passengers as he related to us the tremendous power of this magnificent creation of man.

But power, just like everything else, can be either good or bad. It can be used or misused. This passage singles out the person who has misused his power, one who keeps others down by cruel and unjust means. He rules by harsh tyranny and tramples others underfoot. He is described as "froward," a stubborn, willful, obstinate person who knows it all and who will not be taught by others. He defies both God and man.

Such a person cannot be envied, but must be pitied, because he is in a headlong plunge toward self-destruction. God resists him and when he fights with God, it is a fight he is sure to lose. His ways are an abomination to the Lord. In contrast, those to be envied are the saints of God who are walking quietly with the Lord.

They have a secret the world cannot really know. Jesus said, " 'He that hath My commandments, and keepeth them, he it is that loveth Me: and he that loveth Me shall be loved of My Father, and I will love him, and will manifest Myself to him.' Judas saith unto Him, not Iscariot, 'Lord, how is it that Thou will manifest Thyself to us, and not unto the world?' Jesus answered and said unto him, 'If a man love Me, he will keep My words; and My Father will love him, and We will come unto him, and make our abode with him' " (John 14:21-23).

Those saints of God are in moment-by-moment communion with God. Their lives are filled with a peace that the world cannot comprehend. Paul stated, "Be careful for nothing; but in everything by prayer and supplication with thanksgiving let your requests be made known unto God. And the peace of God, which passeth all understanding, shall keep your hearts and minds through Christ Jesus" (Phil. 4:6-7).

It is possible for them to maintain a spirit of joy, to "rejoice in the Lord always" (Phil. 4:4), because the joy of the Lord is firmly fixed in their lives. "These things have I spoken unto you, that My joy might remain in you, and that your joy might be full (John 15:11).

The Lord communicates His truth to their hearts. In His prayer, Jesus said, "I thank Thee, O Father, Lord of heaven and earth, because Thou hast hid these things from the wise and prudent, and hast revealed them unto babes" (Matt. 11:25).

And despite all outward appearances, they have the assurance that behind it all is the loving hand of God. "Whoso is wise, and will observe these things, even they shall understand the lovingkindness of the Lord" (Ps. 107:43). It is truly more satisfying to dwell on the high hill of God's blessing than amid the vanity and pomp of this world.

"The curse of the Lord is in the house of the wicked, but He blesseth the habitation of the just. Surely He scorneth the scorners, but He giveth grace unto the lowly. The wise shall inherit glory, but shame shall be the promotion of fools" (3:33-35).

The last three verses of this passage present three contrasts between the wise man and the fool. It is the pattern of the Book of Proverbs to set against one another the behavior of the righteous and the behavior of the sinner. Through the use of a common and very effective device in Hebrew poetry, that of antithetical parallelism, Solomon vividly contrasts the just, the lowly, and the wise with the wicked, the scorner, and the fool.

Have you ever wondered what it would be like to know that you were under a terrible curse? And worse yet, to know that you were under the curse of Almighty God? Today, millions of hopeless people around the world live in mortal fear of a hateful, mean, ugly god who is constantly devising evil against them. Daily they offer chants, burn incense, and perform rituals. Deep in their hearts they know it is all in vain, yet they continue.

I have talked with people who had lived in constant fear of death and destruction, but who were delivered into the light of the grace of the true and living God. After their conversions, they could lie down and sleep in peace. They no longer feared the demons who had oppressed them for most of their lives. The devil indeed is a hard taskmaster.

The first of these contrasts speaks of actually having the curse of God on the house of the wicked. A number of times Scripture paints this picture for us. One concerns the children of Israel during their wanderings in the wilderness. God had "saved them from the hand of him that hated them, and redeemed them from the hand of the enemy" (Ps. 106:10).

But then a strange thing happened. "They soon forgot His works; they waited not for His counsel, but lusted exceedingly in the wilderness, and tempted God in the desert" (Ps. 106:13-14). They grew weary of the food God had provided. "And the mixed multitude that was among them fell a-lusting; and the children of Israel also wept again, and said, 'Who shall give us flesh to eat? We remember the fish, which we did eat in Egypt freely; the cucumbers, and the melons, and the leeks, and the onions, and the garlic; but now our soul is dried away; there is nothing at all, beside this manna, before our eyes' " (Num. 11:4-6).

In response to their demands, God gave them what they asked for. "He gave them their request; but sent leanness into their soul" (Ps. 106:15).

No doubt they felt they had forced the hand of God, had made Him bow to their demands. They thought they had won. They had done battle with God and had defeated Him. With jutted jaws, heads held high, chests out, and smiles on their lips, they strutted about the camp, little realizing that they were living under the curse of God. Their stomachs became fat, but leanness entered their souls. Their physical appetites were satisfied, but their spirits dried up. Centuries later the prophet recorded God speaking, " ' If ye will not hear, and if ye will not lay it to heart, to give glory unto My name,' saith the Lord of hosts, 'I will even send a curse upon you, and I will curse your blessings; yea, I have cursed them already, because ye do not lay it to heart' " (Mal. 2:2).

The New Testament also speaks of the curse of God. The Apostle Paul had gone into Galatia to preach the Gospel. Many had responded in that area to the free gift of life in Jesus Christ and had given their lives to Him. However, there followed on the heels of the apostle some who had perverted the truth of Christ by adding the burden of works to the glorious free salvation. The Apostle Paul, because of his own background as a Pharisee of the Pharisees, knew the horror of living under the curse of the law.

Paul, knowing that the end of salvation by works was the way of death said, "I marvel that ye are so soon removed from Him that called you into the grace of Christ unto another gospel: which is not another; but there be some that trouble you, and would pervert the Gospel of Christ. But though we, or an angel from heaven, preach any other gospel unto you than that which we have preached unto you, let him be accursed. As we said before, so say I now again, if any man preach any other gospel unto you than that ye have received, let him be accursed" (Gal. 1:6-9).

The apostle knew that his message had come directly from the risen Christ. "But I certify you, brethren, that the Gospel which was preached of me is not after man. For I neither received it of man, neither was I taught it, but by the revelation of Jesus Christ" (Gal. 1:11-12).

But the contrast is always there—God blesses the "habitation of the just." In Old Testament times, God gave His people a choice, "See, I have set before thee this day life and good, and death and evil; in that I command thee this day to love the Lord thy God, to walk in His ways, and to keep His commandments and His statutes and His judgments, that thou mayest live and multiply; and the Lord thy God shall bless thee in the land whither thou goest to possess it. . . . I call heaven and earth to record this day against you, that I have set before you life and death, blessing and cursing: therefore choose life, that both thou and thy seed may live" (Deut. 30:15-16, 19).

Those who choose life, living according to the commandments of God, are those who dwell in the "habitation of the just." On the other hand, those who choose death and rebel against God and His holy law, are those who are part of the "house of the wicked," and the curse of God abides on them.

Those who choose death are also called scorners. I was touring a palace in Yogyakarta, Indonesia on one of my trips, when the guide pointed out a picture of one of the ancient kings of that land; the eyes of his portrait seemed to follow me around the chamber. I went to the far left and to the far right of the huge room, and he still seemed to gaze directly at me. It gave me an eerie feeling.

The scorner must feel that way at times. It is abundantly evident in the Bible that God resists the proud and sets Himself against the rebels in this world. He literally scorns the scorners. He did so at the Tower of Babel. The people of that time had decided to build a city and a tower that, through their own efforts, would reach to heaven itself. The Lord took note of this willful demonstration of pride, arrogance, and scorn, and put a quick stop to it (Gen. 10—11).

On another occasion, Pharaoh decided to ignore the vivid lessons of the 10 plagues, and pursued the fleeing Israelites with 600 chosen charioteers. He was going to make war on God and His people, but the results were quite unexpected. The Lord overthrew the Egyptians in the midst of the sea, "And the waters returned, and covered the chariots, and the horsemen, and all the host of Pharaoh that came into the sea after them; there remained not so much as one of them" (Ex. 14:28). The scorn and contempt for God that filled the heart of Pharaoh as he mocked and ridiculed the God of Israel finally caught up with him. He ate the fruit of his own planting, and perished in the sea under the scorn of God.

Sennacherib was a mighty and exalted Assyrian king who also tried to scorn God and His people. He had come up against the land of Judah and attempted to capture and destroy its capital city, Jerusalem, as he had other cities before it. He sent word to its inhabitants that it would be utter nonsense to try to prevent him from taking the city. He warned them not to be foolish, particularly not to believe that their God could possibly help them. His exact words were, "He shall not be able to deliver you" (Isa. 36:14).

When Hezekiah received these scornful demands for unconditional surrender, he took it to the Lord in prayer, "O

Lord of hosts, God of Israel, that dwellest between the cherubim, Thou art the God, even Thou alone, of all the kingdoms of the earth: Thou hast made heaven and earth. Incline Thine ear, O Lord, and hear; open Thine eyes, O Lord, and see: and hear all the words of Sennacherib, which hath sent to reproach the living God. . . . Now therefore, O Lord our God, save us from his hand, that all the kingdoms of the earth may know that Thou art the Lord, even Thou only" (37:16-17, 20).

God answered by utterly destroying the Assyrian host, and once again the scorner tasted the fruit of his own planting. By way of contrast, the lowly were delivered through the grace of the Lord. They had depended on Him, and He had answered them.

The Pharisees who resisted the teachings of Jesus Christ and who tried to heap ridicule and scorn on Him also tasted the fruit of their planting. Jesus prophesied, "Therefore say I unto you, the kingdom of God shall be taken from you, and given to a nation bringing forth the fruits thereof" (Matt. 21:43).

But God's love and grace is showered on the ones who are contrite in spirit and lowly in heart. Note the example of the Roman soldier who came to Jesus with a prayer for his sick servant. "Jesus saith unto him, 'I will come and heal him.' The centurion answered and said, 'Lord, I am not worthy that Thou shouldest come under my roof; but speak the word only, and my servant shall be healed' " (Matt. 8:7-8).

The publican who prayed in repentant humility received forgiveness for his sins and was declared justified in the sight of God. In all ages, the declaration of God is clear, "Thus saith the High and Lofty One that inhabiteth eternity, whose name is Holy, 'I dwell in the high and holy place, with him also that is of a contrite and humble spirit, to revive the spirit of the humble, and to revive the heart of the contrite ones' " (Isa. 57:15).

Contrary to current popular opinion, the meek shall inherit the earth. Why? Because God has said so—He gives grace to the lowly. But the bloated soul, bristling with its own importance, has no room for the humbling grace of God. The humble spirit gladly exchanges the puny, rotten little idol of self for the presence of the One who alone has the right to rule in the hearts of men.

Another description of the lowly person, one who is just in the sight of God, is that he is wise. And that is in contrast with those designated as fools. The wise man inherits glory; the fool shame.

In many of our lives there are times of anticipation that are almost beyond our ability to bear. Christmastime is like that for children. They wonder what's in those packages with their names on them; they can hardly wait to open their presents and their expectations know no bounds. The young woman who has fallen in love with a young man has the same keen sense of anticipation as she hopes for the day that her beloved will pop the question and slip a ring on her finger.

This last contrasting statement in verse 35 has two words in it that call forth such emotion and excitement. The first word speaks of the person who is expecting an *inheritance*. The person knows it is coming and can hardly sleep. How much will it be? When will it arrive? What shall I do with it? Little else is on the person's mind as he anticipates its arrival.

The other word is *promotion*. Here again we have a word that puts a person on the edge of his chair. Am I about to be promoted? What will my new responsibilities be? What kind of salary goes with it? Will I like my new job? Will I be able to handle it?

The last verse of this chapter also speaks of the fool. A fool is not a person of limited mental capacity, but one who has, by his own will and in spite of his better judgment, denied God. The psalmist speaks of such a man in Psalms 14 and 53. Both begin with the same words, "The fool hath said in his heart, 'There is no God.' " The fool who says this is the scorner, the blasphemer, the proud, the arrogant, the one who walks through the earth mocking the Almighty and any who trust in Him.

By way of contrast, this verse also speaks of the wise man. Again, this is not necessarily the man with great mental capacity or high IQ, but it is the person who is walking in submission to the good, acceptable, and perfect will of God. So Solomon has been teaching and contrasting in this Book of Proverbs. In this great body of believers, you will find some of the great men of the world and some of the lowly. You will find the president of a great university and the groundskeeper of that same institution. They are brothers in Christ who follow the Lord totally.

Two other contrasting words in verse 35 are *shame* and *glory*. The Book of Daniel elaborates on this thought: "Many of them that sleep in the dust of the earth shall awake, some to everlasting life, and some to shame and everlasting contempt. And they that be wise shall shine as the brightness of the firmament; and they that turn many to righteousness as the stars for ever and ever" (Dan. 12:2-3).

The inheritance of the wise, the lowly, and the just is beyond words. This person will experience the unlimited knowledge of God. On the other hand, the promotion that awaits the fool, the scorner, and the wicked is eternal shame. An illustration of the latter is the wicked and treacherous Haman, who was hanged on the high gallows and became a gazingstock to the world (Es. 7:10).

All these exhortations show the righteous or wise person as the one who walks with God in a close relationship. The psalmist speaks of such a person: "A day in Thy courts is better than a thousand. I had rather be a doorkeeper in the house of my God, than to dwell in the tents of wickedness. For the Lord God is a sun and shield: the Lord will give grace and glory; no good thing will He withhold from them that walk uprightly. O Lord of hosts, blessed is the man that trusteth in Thee" (Ps. 84:10-12).

7

"Wisdom Is the Principal Thing"

Proverbs 4:1-19

The wise person has to make some vital choices in order to walk humbly with his God. In the next two sections of the Book of Proverbs, Solomon discusses certain characteristics and motives that must be a part of a person's behavior pattern throughout his lifetime. The person must choose to accept responsibility for maintaining fellowship with God.

Solomon continues to use the device of a father addressing his children in the use of "ye children" (Prov. 4:1) and "my son" (4:10), including in this passage a third generation of relationships in mentioning his parents (4:3). The point is that the best climate for the transmission of these truths is in the family situation, where the ties of affection are strongest. The approach is positive, for the committed learner is not shown a series of negatives but the kind of life that really reflects the best in this world. As the heart of all this is wisdom, for it is "the principal thing" (4:7).

The second section contrasts the two paths, a theme Solomon has been pursuing in his previous teachings (Prov. 1—3). Here the way of wisdom (4:10-13) is set forth against the path of wickedness (4:14-17), with two paths compared at the end (4:18-19). The challenge is for us to choose the way of the wise.

"Hear, ye children, the instruction of a father, and attend to know understanding. For I give you good doctrine; forsake ye not my law" (4:1-2).

Some years ago we were trying to lay some ground rules for the selection of staff for our Navigators' boys camp at Eagle Lake in Colorado. Lorne Sanny, president of The Navigators, was chairing the meeting. After he had heard all the suggestions as to the kinds of men who should serve as counselors, water safety people, teachers of crafts, marksmanship, and archery, Lorne added one thing.

"It seems to me we should make sure we have a couple of men at the camp who have raised some boys," "They would understand and be a bit more sympathetic to things like homesickness and loneliness. They would be able to supply the added ingredient of patience and understanding when fear or an upset stomach or a blister makes life hard for the boys."

That's an extremely important point. We needed to make sure all the technical skills were present at the camp. But having a dad on hand who had raised boys of his own would certainly add another dimension that all the training in camping and counseling could never provide.

In this passage, Solomon does not speak as an eminent patron of the arts, nor as a learned zoologist, botanist, or astronomer. He speaks as a father. So the wisdom he shares is not based on the educational or scientific scale of life, but comes from the warm, loving, wise, and tender heart of a father to his children.

A father is certainly concerned about the education of his children. He would delight to have his son or daughter conversant with Shelley, Keats, and Tennyson, understand and appreciate the paintings of Michelangelo and Reubens, able to quote and discuss Shakespeare and Longfellow, and be a master in calculus, trigonometry, and algebra. But if you ask that father about his praying for his children, he will tell you that he prays that they will be well-behaved boys and girls, who will grow up to be good, kind, loving, and morally upright men and women.

The father is *concerned* about the education of their minds, but he is burdened for the goodness and purity of their hearts and lives. He calls on them to hear and attend to the good teaching (doctrine) he will teach and the law he will lay before them.

The law, no doubt, is the law of God, for after all, it is obedience to the law of the Lord that brings freedom to our lives. Freedom is the power to do what you ought, not the license to do what you will. The most relaxed man at the banquet is the one who understands and has mastered the rules of etiquette perfectly. He is at ease, poised, and does what is right by second nature. The one who is unlearned in the graces of table manners and good etiquette is always on edge, wondering which fork to use, which plate to use for what, and which glass is the proper one.

It goes without saying, then, that the instruction of the father is for the good of the child. In spite of replies like, "But, Dad, everybody's doing it," and, "Everybody thinks this way," he sticks with truth and sound teaching based on the Word of God. That is the way of wisdom that a father is responsible to pass on to his children.

"For I was my father's son, tender and only beloved in the sight of my mother. He taught me also, and said unto me, 'Let thine heart retain my words: keep my commandments, and live. Get wisdom, get understanding: forget it not; neither decline from the words of my mouth. Forsake her not, and she shall preserve thee: love her, and she shall keep thee. Wisdom is the principal thing; therefore get wisdom: and with all thy getting get understanding. Exalt her, and she shall promote thee: she shall bring thee to honor, when thou dost embrace her. She shall give to thine head an ornament of grace: a crown of glory shall she deliver to thee' " (4:3-9).

In this remarkable passage we are taken into the very heart of David, the man after God's own heart. Solomon tells us what his father passed on to him, and this gives us another glimpse into the character of this man of God. When we think of David, various events usually come to mind. We see him as a shepherd boy on the slopes around Bethlehem tending his sheep; we see him facing the lion and the bear that would threaten his flock. We see him approaching the giant Goliath with a few stones to do battle with that loud, powerful, well-trained warrior of the Philistines. We see him in the palace of Saul, playing his harp and singing the songs that soothed the troubled spirit of the first king of Israel. We see him as the commander of the army and the king of the nation. We see him as the "sweet singer of Israel," author of many of the psalms. We see him, finally, as an old and feeble man praying on his deathbed for his successor, Solomon.

But how often do we see David in the setting of his own home, relaxing by the fire, instructing his son? That's the picture Solomon gives us in this passage. It is obvious from what we read here that David loved Solomon as his own soul and spent much time with him to impress on him the necessity of applying himself to the search for wisdom and understanding.

We also gain insight into the soul of Solomon. When he was grown, he enjoyed sharing with others what his father had shared with him. This is a beautiful thing to see in the life of a man who is noted for his wisdom. Too often, after a young man has achieved some success in his field, he seems to be ashamed of the low estate of his parents.

A magazine once told of a famous musician who refused to perform in a certain city. No one knew the reason for that till someone discovered that it was the home of his parents. They were simple, ordinary folk, and he was afraid that they would come to his concert and embarrass him. He did not want his friends to meet his humble mom and dad, yet they were the ones who had paid for his music lessons!

Through the instruction of his father, Solomon had learned the necessity of passing along to others what he had learned. This applied to spiritual children as well. We are reminded of Paul's words to Timothy, "Thou therefore, my son, be strong in the grace that is in Christ Jesus. And the things that thou hast heard of me among many witnesses, the same commit thou to faithful men, who shall be able to teach others also" (2 Tim. 2:1-2).

It is clear that what David had told his son was true. It had come to pass: wisdom was what made Solomon the man he was. As long as he pursued her (in Proverbs wisdom is personified as a woman), the blessings of doing things God's way were his. When he got wisdom, he got understanding; as long as he went after her, she preserved him and kept him (Prov. 4:6). As long as he exalted and embraced her, she promoted him and brought him honor.

The promotion was the position of honor and esteem that Solomon had before others. His glory was spread abroad and his wisdom was the wonder of that part of the world. He had listened to the words of his father. He had retained his words in his heart, had not declined from or forgotten them, and had not forsaken the instructions he had received as a youth.

These blessings can be ours as well. The older we grow the more we acknowledge the fact that our parents knew what they were talking about. What they taught was right. It came from the Lord and was based on a lifetime of experience. Solomon had learned his lesson well, and was now passing it on to his children.

"Hear, O my son, and receive my sayings; and the years of thy life shall be many. I have taught thee in the way of wisdom; I have led thee in right paths. When thou goest, thy steps shall not be straitened; and when thou runnest, thou shalt not stumble. Take fast hold of instruction; let her not go: keep her; for she is thy life" (4:10-13).

Our contemporary age has much to say about defense systems. Congress debates about the best and surest means of protecting the country. Various burglar alarm systems are being sold as the way of protecting homes against those who would plunder them. People purchase dogs trained to guard property. Vitamins and health foods are sold to guard against disease and infirmity. When travelers go overseas, they are required to have certain shots to protect them from the ravages of peculiar diseases and various jungle fevers. The makers of mouthwashes vie for our affections by assuring us that theirs tastes better and lasts longer than the competition, thus protecting us from offending our neighbors with our breath.

In this passage, Solomon looks on wisdom as a defense system. He says that our lives will not be hemmed in, restricted, or confined; they will be broadened and their range made much greater. When we run through life prepared, we will not stumble.

Many of us have read of the desperate plight of families leaving Oklahoma, during the days when that state was a great dustbowl, to go to California with the hope of bettering themselves. On arrival there, they found themselves in even greater difficulties. They had no friends, no money, no way to make a decent living. Then men had no education or skills with which to land jobs. Their diet was limited to a few scraps of food; their living quarters were narrow and cramped. The jobs that the men could find were limited to those being sought by hundreds of others also in desperate situations.

Solomon reminds us that a good education will relieve us from worry about how to survive, and will open doors of opportunity to a wider and broader life. If we diligently search for wisdom, study hard in school, and learn what we can in our youth, these things will help us in our later years from being confined to a narrow and restricted lifestyle.

The last verse in this section takes on an urgent note in the use of a rapid succession of verbs: *Take hold, let her not go, keep her.* These apply to the whole area of advancement in life. Many of us may know of a young person who started out well and never achieved much afterward. When opportunities for promotion came along, others were chosen because they had applied themselves to learning what was necessary for that particular job.

The young person who idles away his or her time, who plays while others hit the books, will eventually regret that slothfulness. But the opposite of that is diligence—applying oneself to wisdom. When you do that, you won't live a restricted life, and you won't stumble when the opportunities for progress present themselves. This is tremendous advice to the young man or young woman who would like to have his or her life really count for God in his or her chosen field of earnest endeavor.

"Enter not into the path of the wicked, and go not in the way of evil men. Avoid it, pass not by it, turn from it, and pass away. For they sleep not, except they have done mischief; and their sleep is taken away, unless they cause some to fall. For they eat the bread of wickedness, and drink the wine of violence" (4:14-17).

What is it that causes a person to choose a life of sin? Is it a lack of knowledge? Is it that he just doesn't know any better? David once asked, "Have all the workers of iniquity no knowledge, who eat up my people as they eat bread, and call not upon the Lord?" (Ps. 14:4)

No, the problem is not a lack of knowledge, but a lack of moral conviction. These people actually enjoy their chosen way of life and that enjoyment is heightened when they are successful in leading others into their perverted life-styles. Jesus said that the thing which sustained Him in life—His meat—was "to do the will of Him that sent Me and finish His work" (John 4:34). The bread and drink of those who want to do evil is wickedness and violence. Their wickedness stems from their dedication, ultimately, to the evil one.

In answering the accusations of His enemies, Jesus told them, "Verily, verily, I say unto you, whosoever committeth sin is the servant of sin. . . . Ye are of your father the devil, and the lusts of your father ye will do. He was a murderer from the beginning, and abode not in the truth, because there is no truth in him. When he speaketh a lie, he speaketh of his own, for he is a liar, and the father of it" (John 8:34, 44).

Now that poses a serious problem for the person who is in that predicament. If the basic premise of his life is wrong, nothing that you add to it will be right. If he wants to go north but is going south, nothing he says or does will make any difference. He will still arrive at the wrong destination. The only thing that can possibly help would be a complete turnaround—to stop going south and start going north.

That is what the Bible's teaching on repentance is all about—a complete change of direction. But the mind of the person who is committed to evil as a way of life is so closed to instruction and advice that the problem seems hopeless. And, humanly speaking, it is. But thank God for the power of His grace, mercy, and love as it is communicated through the Gospel by the Holy Spirit. He is able to get through and enable a person to repent—to turn around.

The wicked in this passage are following the same pattern of the wicked one whom they follow. First of all, the devil sinned as he rebelled against God. His second act was to tempt others to sin also. And here we see these workers of iniquity pursuing their ungodly ways with sleepless zeal.

The psalmist described this kind of evil worked with amazing accuracy: "The transgression of the wicked saith within my heart, that there is no fear of God before his eyes. For he flattereth himself in his own eyes, until his iniquity he found to be hateful. The words of his mouth are iniquity and deceit: he hath left off to be wise, and do good. He deviseth mischief upon his bed; he setteth himself in a way that is not good; he abhorreth not evil" (Ps. 36:1-4).

Centuries later, the Apostle Peter gave us this vivid description of these evil ones: "But these, as natural brute beasts, made to be taken and destroyed, speak evil of the things that they understand not; and shall utterly perish in their own corruption. . . . Having eyes full of adultery, and that cannot cease from sin; beguiling unstable souls: an heart they have exercised with covetous practices; cursed children: which have forsaken the right way, and are gone astray, following the way of Balaam the son of Bosor, who loved the wages of unrighteousness. . . . These are wells without water, clouds that are carried with a tempest; to whom the mist of darkness is reserved forever" (2 Peter 2:12, 14-15, 17).

The Prophet Micah wrote: "Woe to them that devise iniquity, and work evil upon their beds! When the morning is light, they practice it, because it is the power of their hand" (Micah 2:1). Would to God that the followers of Jesus Christ were as motivated with a holy zeal to do good as these workers of iniquity are motivated to do evil.

Would to God that our hearts and words were taken up with devising ways and means to get the message of life and hope to a world in desperate need. Bishop Wood of the Church of England said, "There is no greater good you and I can do to any other contemporary of ours than to speak to him of Jesus and lead him to a knowledge of Jesus Christ as Lord."

The psalmist stated, "The wicked, through the pride of his countenance, will not seek after God: God is not in all his thoughts" (Ps. 10:4). That means only one thing: We must take the positive action of taking the knowledge of God to him. Jesus told His disciples to go, and we must do just that.

Today the world is saturated with the undisguised maligning

of sin as it injects its venom into the veins of unsuspecting youth. We must be diligent to plant in their hearts and minds the life-changing message of Jesus Christ. He alone has the power to protect, the power to thwart the attacks of the enemy, and power to place them safely on the path of righteousness.

"But the path of the just is as the shining light, that shineth more and more unto the perfect day. The way of the wicked is as darkness: they know not at what they stumble" (4:18-19).

My family and I enjoy visiting my wife's mother, for her home is nestled among some trees up against a high bluff. One night my son Randy and I decided to climb the stairs that go to the top of a steep enbankment. We discovered about one third of the way up that some of the wooden steps had rotted away, and it was too dark to see where we were stepping. So we decided to go back down lest we twist our ankles or fall and hurt ourselves. The next morning I took another look at the steps and discovered that it was relatively easy to avoid the dangers. The difference was that now there was enough light to see what was there.

This passage uses this same picture to show the contrast between the path of the one who is walking with God and one who is not. The light that shines on the path of the child of God is the brilliant illumination of God Himself. His light is not the dim and feeble light of the human candles of the wisdom of this world. These do not give much light and are easily extinguished. Nor is it the sudden brilliance of a falling star, a momentary light that is extinguished almost as soon as it is seen.

The light that God provides is His Word. The hymn writer James H. Sammis put it this way:

When we walk with the Lord
In the light of His Word,
What a glory He sheds on our way:
While we do His good will,
He abides with us still,
And with all who will trust and obey.

In this passage Solomon also points out the progressive growth of the soul. At first the new disciple may struggle with past sins which cast long shadows along the way. He may struggle with the temptation to put his own wisdom ahead of the wisdom of God. He may struggle with the vestiges of his own righteousness as opposed to relying completely on the righteousness of Christ.

But growth in grace brings release from the dark shackles of the past, and he bursts forth into the glorious light of God. Old habits, old associations, old ways, give way to the good, acceptable, and perfect will of God. So the light shines more and more into his life.

This is pictured for us by the experience of the blind man of Bethsaida when he met Jesus. "They bring a blind man unto Him, and besought Him to touch him. And He took the blind man by the hand, and led him out of the town; and when He had spit on his eyes, and put His hands upon him, He asked him if he saw aught. And he looked up and said, 'I see men as trees, walking.' After that He put His hands again upon his eyes, and made him look up; and he was restored, and saw every man clearly" (Mark 8:22-25). This is not the picture of the Christian position, but the Christian walk, as we grow more and more into the likeness of Christ.

The way of the wicked, however, is the path of darkness without the safety, comfort, and direction that comes from walking hand in hand with Jesus Christ. The love of sin turns off the light. The cry of the wicked is heard, "We grope for the wall like the blind, and we grope as if we had no eyes: we stumble at noonday as in the night; we are in desolate places as dead men" (Isa. 59:10).

The Gospel is both the way that leads to Christ and a stumbling-stone to the mind that is set against Him. Paul stated, "Israel, which followed after the law of righteousness, hath not attained to the law of righteousness. Wherefore? Because they sought it not by faith, but as it were by the works of the law. For they stumbled at that stumblingstone; as it is written, 'Behold, I lay in Sion a stumblingstone and rock of offence: and whosoever believeth on Him shall not be ashamed' " (Rom. 9:31-33).

We need to pray as we share Christ with those who are walking in darkness, because the devil has blinded their minds against Christ and the Gospel. Paul wrote, "But if our Gospel be hid, it is hid to them that are lost: in whom the god of this world hath blinded the minds of them which believe not, lest the light of the glorious Gospel of Christ, who is the image of God, should shine unto them" (2 Cor. 4:3-4).

Through prayer we can see that spiritual blindfold removed and rejoice as the person emerges into the light of the Gospel. Through our prayers and actions we can help those who are living in darkness, those who do not even know why they are stumbling, to see that light and begin to walk along the path that leads to a perfect day.

8

Wisdom and Close Relationships

Proverbs 4:20—5:23

Before discussing the closest and most intimate of human relationships—marriage—Solomon prepares the way by challenging his readers and hearers to a spiritual-medical self-examination. If one is to have the right marital relationship, he or she must have settled some basic issues in life. And these issues are a proper relationship with God (earlier teaching by Solomon), and a healthy outlook, attitude, and behavior in relation to other people.

In order to have a biblical and God-blessed marriage, the couple must have examined themselves and made some personal commitments before they can make their commitments to each other. Self-examination has to do with the heart, the mouth, the eyes, and the feet. This foundational section (Prov. 4:20-27) is introduced by the familiar words of the exhortation to listen to the voice of wisdom, for the way we build our spiritual foundations is by careful review of familiar and lasting truths.

Once the foundation of interpersonal relationships is solidly built, then more intimate relationships of marriage can be discussed. So the next section (5:1-23) first warns of the subtle charms of the seductive woman (5:1-6), then gives a stark warning against infidelity (5:7-14), and concludes with the presentation of the wholesomeness of a proper marital relationship in contrast to its awful alternative (5:15-23).

"My son, attend to my words; incline thine ear unto my sayings. Let them not depart from thine eyes; keep them in the midst of thine heart. For they are life unto those that find them, and health to all their flesh" (4:20-22).

At one time or another, most people have bought something from a door-to-door salesman. You may be glad the salesman dropped by if he offered something you needed. You may have bought it if his product was new and revolutionary, and had the promise of making your life better and brighter.

But what if a salesman called and told you something like this: "Here's something that will really help you. When you have a decision to make, it will help you make the right one. It will also warn you of any danger that is lurking nearby, anything that might prove harmful to you or your family. It will help you know what is right, help you avoid that which is wrong, and you can use it to keep out of harm's way."

As you listened to this salesman's pitch, you would probably conclude that his product was too good to be true. And you would most likely be right, unless he was selling the Bible. Then you could buy with perfect confidence, for the wisdom of the Word of God is time-tested and true. It really can provide all those things.

I read once of an African who learned one day that the bookstore in a nearby town would soon receive a shipment of Bibles in his own language. He belonged to a tribe that had never had the Word in its language, and now after many years of labor the translators had completed their work. Excitement mounted as the day approached when the Bibles would arrive. The man could not sleep the night before their arrival; his excitement and anticipation were too great. Early the next morning he walked the eight miles to town to be one of the first to buy a Bible in his own language. He found others there who shared his excitement and anticipation.

The following Sunday the Bibles were brought to the church, and when the people saw the stack of Bibles their joy knew no bounds. They jumped and leaped in the air; they laughed and shouted and sang; they clapped their hands. Then some-one said, "Let us thank God for these Bibles." Right there and then, before the service began, they thanked God for His wonderful provision of the Word in their tongue. These grate-ful people had little difficulty in following Solomon's admoni-tion to "let them not depart from thine eyes; keep them in the midst of they heart" (Prov. 4:21).

Our spiritual lives begin as God the Holy Spirit uses His Word to reveal Jesus Christ to our hearts. Our eyes are opened and we come to Jesus in repentance and faith. Then our spiritual health is nourished and maintained as we feed and feast our souls on that Word. There is enough healing power in the Bible to cure all the spiritual and moral ills of the en-tire world.

As we attend to the words of Scripture and incline our ears attentively to what God has to say to us, we really experience what life—eternal life—is all about in the here and now. Truly, the careful concentration on the Word of God is "life unto those that find them" (4:22).

"Keep thy heart with all diligence; for out of it are the issues of life. Put away from thee a froward mouth, and perverse lips put far from thee. Let thine eyes look right on, and let thine eyelids look straight before thee. Ponder the path of thy feet, and let all thy ways be established. Turn not to the right hand nor to the left; remove thy foot from evil" (4:23-27).

Commitment to the Word of God enables us to conduct our spiritual-medical self-examination, as we evaluate our hearts, mouths, eyes, and feet.

The heart (4:23). The heart can be many things. One songwriter tells us he left his heart in San Francisco; another sings, "My Heart Belongs to Daddy!" A girl named Peg was not just Peg, but "Peg of My Heart." My doctor tells me the heart is merely a pump, but it just doesn't sound right to call Peg "Peg of My Pump," or to tell people "I Left My Pump in San Francisco." So the heart must be more than that alone.

The Scriptures clearly teach that the heart is more than just another part of the human anatomy like a shoulder or an elbow. The Apostle Paul prayed that "Christ may dwell in your hearts by faith" (Eph. 3:17). That important theme is borne out in many other passages.

Biblically the concept seems to speak of the throne room of the inner man. It is the most comprehensive term used for the human personality. In the Book of Proverbs the term *heart* stands for the mind (3:3; 6:21), the emotions (15:15, 30), the will (11:20; 14:14), and the whole inner person (3:5). The Scriptures further state that Jesus Christ Himself must be the One to occupy the central place, the highest place, the place of honor and control—the human heart.

The heart, representing the whole man, has a variety of dangerous and deadly enemies lurking in the shadows, ready at a moment's notice to launch an attack and attempt to take over the government of that person's life. Satan is all too familiar with the sins that so easily beset us and waits to capitalize on any move in their direction.

The world, with its temporal treasures and pleasures, waits to lure us down the forbidden paths of personal gain and glory. The devil constantly flings his fiery darts of doubt to dull our affections for God. The flesh gains strength by feeding on the corruption of greed, envy, lust, and pride, and tries to mobilize an attack along these broad roads that lead to destruction. Thus Solomon's admonition to "keep thy heart with all diligence."

But in the midst of all these dangers listed above, is it really possible for a man to keep his heart with all diligence? Of course not! Only God can do that. Why then the admonition to do so? Because the *desire* to keep his heart and to have a pure, holy, Christ-honoring, Christ-centered life is the *means* by which God guards the godly person and sees him through those dangers. The man who attends to the words of God, inclines his ear to His sayings, and keeps them before him and in him is the one who keeps his heart with all diligence, and is truly alive and spiritually healthy (Prov. 4:20-22).

Jesus taught this important truth on a number of occasions, particularly when He referred to what comes out of man (see Mark 7:15-23; Luke 6:45; John 4:14; 7:38). These teachings may have been allusions to this passage in the Book of Proverbs.

Paul also had something to say on this subject—our keeping and God working—when he said, "Wherefore, my beloved, as ye have always obeyed, not as in my presence only, but now much more in my absence, work out your own salvation with fear and trembling. For it is God which worketh in you both to will and to do of His good pleasure" (Phil. 2:12-13).

Jude's conclusion of his brief letter is striking: "Keep yourselves in the love of God, looking for the mercy of our Lord Jesus Christ unto eternal life. . . . Now unto Him that is able to keep you from falling, and to present you faultless before the presence of His glory with exceeding joy, to the only wise God our Saviour, be glory and majesty, dominion and power, both now and forever" (Jude 21, 24-25).

So our dependence on God's keeping power and our diligence in such practical matters as prayer and the devotional life are the keys to the keeping of the heart. The context of this passage has already shown us the need to saturate our lives with the Word by writing it on our hearts through Scripture memory.

We cannot keep our heart, but God can. He waits for our cooperation and obedience to the directions He gives us in His Word. David prayed, "Consider mine enemies, for they are many; and they hate me with cruel hatred. O keep my soul, and deliver me: let me not be ashamed, for I put my trust in Thee" (Ps. 25:19-20).

As we live in an atmosphere of diligent dedication, prayer, and the regular intake of the Word of God, the Spirit of God exercises His control in our hearts and lives. But if the devil can launch an assault and capture our hearts, the whole man is lost—his affections, desires, motives, and goals. So the heart is the center either of sin or of holiness. Jesus taught, "A good man out of the good treasure of the heart bringeth forth good things: and an evil man out of the evil treasure bringeth forth evil things" (Matt. 12:35).

Everything must be kept. Roads, cars, houses, and clothing must be kept and maintained. But most of all, our hearts must be kept, for out of them come all the vital issues of life. *The mouth.* Immediately after the admonition to keep our hearts comes the instruction to guard our lips (4:24). The mark of wisdom is not only *doing* the right thing, but *saying* the right things, not only the right *actions* but the right *answers*.

Here Solomon warns against twisting or distorting the truth. It is a frightening thing to realize that others can be directed along the path of perdition by what we say.

When I was a ticket agent for the Chicago Great Western Railroad, I learned it was far better to give *no* information than to give the *wrong* information.

We must therefore commit both our lives (hearts) and our lips to the keeping power of the Holy Spirit. Jesus taught that if the tree is good, the fruit will be good. But if the tree is corrupt, the fruit will likewise be corrupt. The tree, therefore, is known by its fruit. Jesus stated, "Out of the abundance of the heart the mouth speaketh" (Matt. 12:34). Our words reveal what is in our hearts. Remember then the words of James, "For in many things we offend all. If any man offend not in word, the same is a perfect man, and able also to bridle the whole body" (James 3:2).

The prayer of David is a pattern for us all, "Set a watch, O Lord, before my mouth; keep the door of my lips." "Let the words of my mouth, and the meditation of my heart, be acceptable in Thy sight, O Lord, my strength, and my redeemer" (Pss. 141:3; 19:14). But after having prayed, we must deliberately make the effort to put away from us the froward mouth and perverse lips.

The eyes. After the mouth come the eyes (4:25). Jesus declared, "The light of the body is in the eye; if therefore thine eye be single, thy whole body shall be full of light. But if thine eye be evil, thy whole body shall be full of darkness. If therefore the light that is in thee be darkness, how great is that darkness" (Matt. 6:22-23). The eyes are one of the main highways for sin to enter our hearts. Daily our society bombards us with clever and interesting material from TV, motion pictures, books, and magazines. Much of what they pander spews out from the very pit of hell. The devil's crowd labors day and night to corrupt the hearts and souls of men by releasing tons of filth into the mainstream of literature and entertainment.

This is not a new tactic. In the Garden of Eden, Eve first *saw* that the tree was good, pleasant to the eyes (Gen. 3:6). Peter speaks of those who have eyes full of adultery that cannot cease from sin (2 Peter 2:14). The psalmist prayed,

"Turn away mine eyes from beholding vanity, and quicken Thou me in Thy way" (Ps. 119:37).

As a young man on a farm in Iowa, I learned the importance of keeping my eyes on my work. If I gazed around while riding the horse-drawn cultivator in the corn field, I would do more harm than good. I would not cultivate the corn; I would kill it. I had to keep my eyes on the row of growing grain. If I failed to do this, I could cover it up when it was small or plow it up the second or third time through the field. What I looked at was crucial to the well-being of the crop.

I saw the same danger years later in a Bible school. I was there for a week of messages in the chapel and for counseling students during their free times. One day I was sitting in the lounge, watching a group of young men. Every time a girl walked by, their eyes became like vertical turn signals, clicking up and down. They were allowing their eyes to be used to stimulate the desires of the flesh and feed their carnal natures. This can be deadly, and many a man has eventually fallen because he let his eyes gaze on that which would lead him into temptation.

So much inflammable material exists in the old nature that it is madness to do anything that can kindle a fire. Achan brought destruction to himself and his family, and tragedy to the whole nation, by falling into this very trap. "When I saw among the spoils a goodly Babylonish garment," he later confessed, "and two hundred shekels of silver, and a wedge of gold of fifty shekels weight, then I coveted them, and took them; and, behold, they are hid in the earth in the midst of my tent, and the silver under it" (Josh. 7:21).

The order here is that first he *saw,* then he *coveted,* then he *took,* and then he tried to cover his sin. It began with his eyes. The only antidote to this is to keep our eyes straight before us on the road of life, fixed on Jesus Christ Himself.
The feet. This section of Proverbs ends with a caution for men to ponder the path of their feet (4:26-27). The idea here is to remove or avoid those obstacles or roadblocks in the path that would hinder our walking in the way of the Lord or those that would divert us into strange and foreign paths. We can be detoured in two ways from the path that God has for us: one is to be bumped from it by the opposition of the enemy,

while the other is to be lured off the path by the devil's temptations. These are obstacles to avoid at all costs.

Frequently in the Book of Proverbs we have been warned about the danger of evil company. We have been told to consent not to the enticements of sinners, but to refrain our feet from their paths. Now these admonitions raise this question: "How are we to win sinners to Christ if we avoid them?"

The Bible teaches us that we are to avoid any associations that weaken or destroy our fellowship with God. So if you are with a person whose mouth is foul and whose life-style is rotten, you must check to see what reactions this prompts in your own heart. If you are burdened for that person, find yourself witnessing to him and praying for him, all is well and good. But if you are with a person or group who follow evil ways and you are intrigued by them, you are in grave danger. If you find their life-style interesting and perhaps adventuresome, and are fascinated by their ways, then get out and the quicker the better. Association with them will dampen your fellowship with God.

A simple guide to determining what you should do is this: put the Word of God on one side of the scale and the proposed action on the other. Does the needle point to the known, revealed will of God, or does it point in the direction of the proposed action? Two questions can help you in this matter: "Is it right?" and "Where will it lead?"

The only way you will be able to tell right from wrong is on the basis of the clear teaching of the Bible. The shifting sand of popular opinion or the rotten formulation of the standards of the world are neither good nor helpful. They change with the wind of the uncertainty of human reason. You can usually determine where a particular act will lead you by simply looking around. The derelicts of this world were once full of the hope, excitement, and adventure of youth. But they chose the path of pleasure and now wallow in the mire of hopelessness. They chose the paths of indolence, tried to find the easy road and now bear the burdens of the bitter betrayal of the promises of the world rather than the bright hope of the promises of the Word of God.

Think seriously about these questions when you choose your companions and the course for your feet: (1) Will it deepen fellowship with God? (2) Is it right? (3) Where will it end? Establish your ways by turning neither to the right nor to the left from the narrow path, and keep your feet from doing evil.

The psalmist warned, "The wicked watcheth the righteous, and seeketh to slay him" (Ps. 37:32), but he also promised to the one whose heart is filled with the Word of God: "The law of his God is in his heart; none of his steps shall slide" (37:31).

"My son, attend unto my wisdom, and bow thine ear to my understanding: that thou mayest regard discretion, and that thy lips may keep knowledge. For the lips of a strange woman drop as an honeycomb, and her mouth is smoother than oil: but her end is bitter as wormwood, sharp as a two-edged sword. Her feet go down to death; her steps take hold on hell. Lest thou shouldest ponder the path of life, her ways are moveable, that thou canst not know them. Hear me now therefore, O ye children, and depart not from the words of my mouth. Remove thy way far from her, and come not nigh the door of her house: lest thou give thine honor unto others, and thy years unto the cruel: lest strangers be filled with thy wealth; and thy labors be in the house of a stranger; and thou mourn at the last, when thy flesh and thy body are consumed, and say, "How have I hated instruction, and my heart despised reproof; and have not obeyed the voice of my teachers, nor inclined mine ear to them that instructed me! I was almost in all evil in the midst of the congregation and assembly' " (5:1-14).

Sugarcoated poison is still poison and will kill just as quickly. It may appear to be something else; people may say it is something else. It may even taste like something else, but it is not. It is still poison. When all is said and done and the final results are in, it's not candy, but poison. It may be sweet to the taste, but it will be bitter to the mind and conscience in the end. It is like a sharp two-edged sword. Whichever side strikes will bring a deadly wound.

No one speaks with more authority and confidence than the person who speaks from experience. The skier can tell you of the thrill of the ski slope; the surfer can relate the excitement of riding the curl of the wave; the fisherman who has caught a marlin or swordfish can talk of the satisfaction of that sea battle.

In this section we have the testimony of a man who had fallen into temptation and had begun to post warnings to those who were coming after him. His message is to his son, but in a large sense he is speaking to the youth of the world. In another book he wrote, "I find more bitter than death the woman, whose heart is snares and nets, and her hands as bands: whoso pleaseth God shall escape from her, but the sinner shall be taken by her" (Ecc. 7:26).

This passage goes beyond the outward appearance of a charming woman to the exposure of the very heart of the seductress (5:1-6), and then warns about the dangers of infidelity (5:7-14). It does not mince its language, and ought to serve as a warning sign to young and old alike.

One of the prime objectives of Satan is to keep our minds off the vital issues of life and to keep us enamored with the pleasures of sin. He does his best to keep us caught up in the passing parade of the temporal and to keep our minds off the eternal joys that can be found only in Jesus Christ.

The devil has many allies who propagate his lies and deceit. If it is true that we live but for a moment, we might as well enjoy our sins. If it is true that there is not life after death, we might as well get as much fun and pleasure out of this life as possible. If it is true that there is no God to judge our sins, why be concerned? Just enjoy life.

This humanistic philosophy is continually propagated in the classrooms of our universities and colleges. Eat, drink, and be merry, for tomorrow it all ends. Sounds reasonable, doesn't it? But there is one flaw: "As it is appointed unto men once to die, but after this the judgment" (Heb. 9:27). There *is* life after death; there *is* a God who will judge the world in righteousness and justice.

One of the dangers of being merry—finding physical pleasure—is falling to the seductions of the opposite sex. Since the passage is addressed to Solomon's son, it warns against the wiles of an outwardly appealing woman, the seductress. But it would apply equally as a warning to a daughter against the seduction by a "strange" man.

The advice given by Solomon is sound: when faced with this temptation, the young person must run. Flee! Get away! That is the way to handle sexual temptation. It is to be avoided like we would avoid a street that rabid dogs prowl. Solomon states that if a person falls into this sin, he (or she) will be giving his honor to others. The records of today speak vividly of this fact. Men in high places have fallen from their pinnacles of power into the rotten, polluted, hog wallows of shame. Even congressmen have been affected. Their honor and reputation are gone; they have been ruined, just as Solomon predicted nearly 3,000 years ago, because they are people who won't control themselves.

To look on this sexual temptation lightly is to cast the Bible into the face of God. Throughout His Word He warns of this sin over and over again. We would do well to heed the warning carefully. Examples of it are so numerous that they need not be listed. Just the sin of David with Bathsheba should stand as a grim warning of the horror of this sin in the sight of God and the terrible consequences of it in this life.

Solomon not only speaks of the judgment to come, but also of the way this sin affects our lives. Strong words such as worm-wood, a two-edged sword, death, and hell are used as results of having fallen into this temptation (5:4-5). Perhaps an allusion to some physical results is referred to in the statement that the flesh and the body are consumed (5:11). The whole passage speaks of the shame to which this sin can take men and women.

It all begins when the words of instruction are ignored, when the wisdom and understanding of the Word of God that lead to discretion and knowledge are not regarded (5:1-2). When the Scripture is not listened to and not put into the heart (5:7). When instruction is hated, reproof despised, godly teachers disobeyed, and the ears closed to God's Word (5:12-13). It is a terrible price to pay for disobedience and rebellion.

"Drink waters out of thine own cistern, and running waters out of thine own well. Let thy foundations be dispersed abroad, and rivers of waters in the streets. Let them be only thine own, and not strangers' with thee. Let thy fountain be blessed, and

rejoice with the wife of thy youth. Let her be as the loving hind and pleasant roe; let her breasts satisfy thee at all times; and be thou ravished always with her love. And why wilt thou, my son, be ravished with a strange woman, and embrace the bosom of a stranger? For the ways of man are before the eyes of the Lord, and He pondereth all his goings. His own iniquities shall take the wicked himself, and he shall be holden with the cords of his sins. He shall die without instruction, and in the greatness of his folly he shall go astray" (5:15-23).

Solomon continues by urging his son and all readers to follow the better path of fidelity within marriage. He extols the virtues of a good wife. The joys of one's own home, like the waters of one's own well, are clean, pure, refreshing, and wholesome. The Apostle Paul likens the relationship of Christ and His Church to that of the husband and wife. That in itself should give us the clear direction we need in matters of honor and faithfulness in marriage. The Church is to keep herself only unto Jesus Christ. And the love that the Lord has for His Church is deep, sacrificial, and eternal.

We live in strange and wicked times. Not only is fidelity in marriage brought into question and mocked, but the concept of marriage itself is derided and labeled obsolete. Many have publicly advocated the idea of abandoning the institution of marriage altogether. Unfortunately these are the people who have captured the ears of our youth through their appeal in the media of TV, motion pictures, music, and writing.

Many of these purveyors of the "new morality" have become celebrities through their abilities to entertain. The unfortunate thing is that they then urge their fans and followers to take on their own polluted life-styles. They scoff at the idea of a lifetime commitment to one person. They advocate that people live together if they want to, and because there is no commitment to such an arrangement, walk out when they grow tired of one another's company.

The rising generation of youngsters, reared in the climate of the "new morality," shows the tragic results of lawlessness in violence, rebellion, confusion, bloodshed, death, and deep psychological scars. Man in his arrogance and pride thinks he can improve on that which God had instituted, ordained, and promised to bless from the beginning of the human race. So rebellious man struts through the earth, scoffs at the Word of the living God, and smirks at the life-style of his forebears.

Men and women of all ages call on us to cast off our tired old ethics. They advocate a "new morality" which seems to insist that the nation do that which is good while its citizens do that which is evil. They cry for a national morality, decry the sexual excesses of their leaders, but urge on all citizens an individual *immorality*. They build for themselves lavish and beautiful houses, but refuse to instill within their families that which makes a home truly beautiful: love, devotion, sacrifice, kindness, and patience.

They try to substitute the short-lived pleasures of sin for the lasting joy of a life lived in accordance with the Word of God. These abominations are spewed forth with frightening regularity. The magazine and book racks in bookstores, supermarkets, and airports drip with the deadly poison of ungodly minds as pornography runs rampant throughout the nation. The music of the young rebels and the conversation of popular entertainers on national talk shows leave the residue of its scum and filth in the minds of the youth of the land. The courts allow this "freedom," and the degeneration of this country proceeds at a fast pace.

All this happens because the words of Solomon, the Book of Proverbs, and the whole Bible are being ignored. The wise king of Israel begins his instruction with the symbolism of fountains and waters, speaking of the true biblical marriage relationship—one with one "till death do us part!" (5:14-18a) He then describes that relationship in straightforward language (5:18b-19), warns against the stranger again as a contrast to enjoying, growing, and developing intimacy within marriage (5:20), and concludes with a severe warning to the man who would go his own way.

God's ways are still best. The wise man or woman will hear the words of the living God and follow in His ways. "Thou wilt show me the path of life: in Thy presence is fulness of joy; at Thy right hand there are pleasures for evermore" (Ps. 16:11).

9

The Pitfalls When Wisdom Is Absent

Proverbs 6:1-35

Before returning to a discussion of immorality, one of man's greatest problems, Solomon discusses some practical problems that men face in addition to sexual involvement apart from marriage. These problems also may lead to gross sins, unnecessary debts, sloth, improper behavior, and the seven deadly sins (6:1-19). He concludes by discussing the deadly sin of adultery (6:20-35).

These are all pitfalls into which careless men could fall. And they do so because they unwisely disregard the clear instructions of the Word of God. When wisdom is absent from the life of a man or woman, young or old, then it becomes easy for him or her to fall into the traps laid by the devil along the path of life. We should heed carefully the warning given here.

"My son, if thou be surety for thy friend, if thou hast stricken thy hand with a stranger, thou art snared with the words of thy mouth, thou art taken with the words of thy mouth. Do this now, my son, and deliver thyself, when thou art come into the hand of thy friend; go, humble thyself, and make sure thy friend. Give not sleep to thine eyes, nor slumber to thine eyelids. Deliver thyself as a roe from the hand of the hunter, and as a bird from the hand of the fowler" (6:1-5).

We used to have a saying in the Marine Corps that if you wanted to lose a friend just lend him some money. I often watched that simple axiom prove itself true. Some marine would get in over his head in a poker game and start trying to borrow money to pay his debts. Or he would buy something expensive and then when the gambling payments came due, he would make the rounds trying to scrape up enough money from his friends to meet the obligation. Then something would come up that made it impossible for him to pay back his friends. Meanwhile his buddy needed the money to go on leave, and so it went, round and round. Soon the two men who started out as friends became enemies. Sometimes there would be a fight; more often it would result in name-calling and bitterness. It went on all the time.

This passage does not expressly forbid lending money to another, but it does deal with the problem that arises when you have foolishly borrowed too much. The basic idea is to get out from under the weight of the thing as quickly as possible. A heavy debt can bring great distress to a family, and if repayment difficulties occur, it can bring reproach to the family name.

Our culture today is perhaps the best illustration of the whole problem of debt. The greatest misuse of money is the practice of going into debt to purchase something not really needed. Impulse buying on credit! Solomon directs his words primarily to the young, and wisely so. Although many older adults are likewise in need of this advice, the young are particularly easily ensnared by the clever talk of smooth salesmen.

I've watched young men get way over their heads in debt, while they were serving overseas, through the purchase of expensive cameras and ultrasophisticated stereo equipment. Admittedly these items were sold at reduced rates, but there was still the problem of paying for them. Quite frequently a less expensive camera or stereo would have done just as well as those they bought.

Buying cars is another easy way to get into debt. Young men and women are prone to purchase classy, souped-up sports cars, loaded with extras, and then spend years paying for them, while they watch their investment depreciate in value and rust out from under them. The problem with getting the latest thing is that in just a few months it's obsolete or another style has hit the market.

You cannot buy extensively and become rich. Rarely can you save money by spending it quickly. "Buy now and save" is really a contradiction of terms. Admittedly one time may be better than another to purchase something, but the best advice is to let the buyer beware. The world is out to get your hard-earned money which you labored so long to get. Learn to use it wisely; make a practice of paying cash. And, above all, be a cautious lender.

"Go to the ant, thou sluggard; consider her ways, and be wise: which having no guide, overseer, or ruler, provideth her meat in the summer, and gathereth her food in the harvest. How long wilt thou sleep, O sluggard? When wilt thou arise out of thy sleep? Yet a little sleep, a little slumber, a little folding of the hands to sleep: So shall thy poverty come as one that travelleth, and thy want as an armed man" (6:6-11).

I remember the year my son Randy won an ant farm. His class in grade school was selling candy in order to purchase some supplies for their room. That kid who sold the most won an ant farm. Randy really got excited about the project and worked hard. He went door to door; he phoned our friends; he did everything he could think of to sell candy. When he won the prize and brought it home, it provided many hours of lively entertainment for all of us.

An ant is an interesting creature to watch. You are struck immediately with its natural instinct for hard work. It seems always to be carrying something, going somewhere, and doing something. It appears active, alert, productive, and industrious.

This is the creature to which the Lord now sends us to learn how to conduct our daily affairs. He does not send us to the wily fox to learn cunning, nor to the chameleon to learn deception. He sends us to the ant who has no guide to follow, no overseer to evaluate her work, no ruler to keep her at the job, and yet is an insect which works with enthusiasm, skill, and vigor.

Today, it seems that to the average person this idea of hard work is foreign. To get something for nothing is the dream of millions. Once I spoke with a bus driver who had received $100 from his company and had not done any work to earn it. He hadn't driven a bus or sold a ticket, but was the envy of everyone within earshot on that bus. He had obtained something for nothing and become an instant hero. Had he told us how long and hard he had labored and had been paid an honest wage, he would have been considered dumb. Getting something for nothing was considered "cool."

The problem with sloth and indolence is that their reward is certain. The sluggard sleeps, not realizing that lurking nearby is another actor who will soon take center stage. His entrance is sure, and when he makes the scene, he will take over and call the shots. His name is poverty.

The Bible does not look on sloth as a weakness of the human flesh, but as sin. Left unchecked, it grows in strength and soon consumes the life. We must resist it in the strength of the Lord. He will help to overcome the deadly enemy that takes the various forms and affects the body, mind, and spirit. The Apostle Paul stated, "Therefore, my beloved brethren, be ye steadfast, unmoveable, always abounding in the work of the Lord, forasmuch as ye know that your labor is not in vain in the Lord" (1 Cor. 15:58).

"A naughty person, a wicked man, walketh with a froward mouth. He winketh with his eyes, he speaketh with his feet, he teacheth with his fingers; frowardness is in his heart, he deviseth mischief continually; he soweth discord. Therefore shall his calamity come suddenly; suddenly shall he be broken without remedy" (6:12-15).

In a vivid picture with carefully employed words, Solomon speaks of the troublemaker who sows discord among people, with his big mouth, a wink, actions, and even gestures. He could be called "old garbage mouth." The word *froward* means unruly, not easily controlled, stubbornly willful. He has a loud mouth that is filled with filth and corruption. This type of person comes in all shapes, sizes, and ages.

I have a friend in the Air Force who once prayed an unusual prayer. He asked the Lord to give him an opportunity to give his testimony to a movie star. One day it was an-

114 / *Wisdom from Above*

nounced on base that a well-known motion picture personality was coming to the base to discuss the policies of the military with the officers on that base. It was sort of a protest thing on her part, but the base commander gave her the opportunity to share her views.

After she had done her thing, she opened it up for questions. My friend waited awhile, and then asked her for her ideas on how Jesus Christ might fit into all this. She passed over his question quickly and went on to some others. After another half hour, my friend again asked the same question and added the reason for his asking it. It was because Jesus had brought a peace that was genuine and real into his life. He wanted her to comment on his testimony.

Her eyes flashed; her manner changed. From her mouth spewed forth a filthy, obscene, ugly tirade against Jesus Christ and all He stands for. It became obvious to all that behind the facade was an unruly, foul mouth she could not control.

In a gym in Washington, D.C., I passed a group of distinguished, elderly men who were just standing around and talking. They could have been congressmen, senators, judges, and bank presidents. I could hear one saying in a loud voice, "Did you hear the one about the big Texan . . . ?" And out of his mouth flowed a lewd story.

Froward mouths come in all shapes and sizes—business executives, movie stars, whatever. My wife and I were out for a walk and cut through the playground of a nearby elementary school. The children were out for recess. They had picked up the habit of a froward mouth at an early age. Their language was really shocking to our ears.

The antidote for a foul mouth is to consider the words of Jesus, "O generation of vipers, how can ye, being evil, speak good things? For out of the abundance of the heart the mouth speaketh" (Matt. 12:34). And this speaking then leads to the other actions described here—winking, actions, and gestures.

The only way to avoid the judgment spoken of (Prov. 6:15) is to come to Jesus Christ. The first step is to invite Him to come into your life as Saviour and Lord. Then consistently fill your life with the Word of God. Solomon later gives this promise, "Bow down thine ear, and hear the words of the wise, and apply thine heart unto my knowledge. For it is a pleasant thing if thou keep them within thee [Scripture memory]; they shall withal be fitted in thy lips" (Prov. 22:17-18).

When the Word of God has free reign in our lives through Scripture memory, and is deeply buried in our hearts, our mouths will reflect that which is inside of us.

"These six things doth the Lord hate; yea, seven are an abomination unto Him: a proud look, a lying tongue, and hands that shed innocent blood, an heart that deviseth wicked imaginations, feet that be swift in running to mischief, a false witness that speaketh lies, and he that soweth discord among brethren" (6:16-19).

It is a strange and wonderful fact that the unfathomable wrath of God and the immeasurable mercy of God go hand in hand. All of His wrath, every ounce of it, is directed against sin, while at the same instant all of His mercy, every ounce of it, is directed to the sinner. The wrath of God is in no way similar to the rage of man. God's wrath is a settled, steady attitude against sin that leads Him to an unbending and never-ending warfare against it. It is much like the medical team in the remote jungle village, steadily working to eliminate the disease and filth that constantly threaten the lives of the villagers.

In this passage we learn of the seven things that incur the wrath of God and are an abomination to Him. These have historically been called the seven deadly sins.

Pride. Pride in the heart often gives rise to other and equally odious sins against God and against man. Pride is often the spawning ground for a disdain for others that would lead us to treat them with contempt and use them to forward our own arrogant ambitions. Pride is often the basis for rejecting Christ, which leads to eternal separation from God. Pride leads to an unwillingness to humble ourselves under the mighty hand of God to do His will, and so leads us into a life that is far less than the best that God has planned. Is it any wonder that this sin incurs the hatred of God?

Falsehood. The very nature of God is truth. Jesus said, "I am . . . the truth" (John 14:6). The Bible describes God as the One who cannot lie (Num. 23:19). The message of salvation is called "the Word of the truth of the Gospel" (Col. 1:5).

Jesus taught that God's Word is truth (John 17:17). We are admonished to speak the truth in love (Eph. 4:15). Obviously, the lying tongue is listed in this catalogue of sins because it is contrary to everything that is precious to God and profitable for men. It was falsehood that led to Eve's succumbing to the wiles of the liar, the devil. It was a lie that led to the leprosy of Gehazi, the servant of Elisha. It was falsehood that led to the deaths of Ananias and Sapphira.

The last book of the Bible states, "The fearful, and unbelieving, and the abominable, and murderers, and whoremongers, and sorcerers, and idolaters, *and all liars,* shall have their part in the lake which burneth with fire and brimstone: which is the second death" (Rev. 21:8).

Murder. The next deadly sin is murder. Life is sacred to God and His commandment still stands: "Thou shalt not kill" (Ex. 20:13). Jesus told us of the source of that sin, "Ye are of your father the devil, and the lusts of your father ye will do. He was a murderer from the beginning, and abode not in the truth, because there is no truth in him. When he speaketh a lie, he speaketh of his own: for he is a liar, and the father of it" (John 8:44).

Plotting evil. Deep within the heart of man is a laboratory of evil, a hideous chamber teeming with foul imaginations of unrighteousness and thoughts of revenge. The mind of man has certainly devised unspeakable evils. History will not let us forget the awful plots by the Nazis in World War II to eliminate all the Jews. The concentration camps and gas chambers still evoke horror in thinking men who remember that terrible period as "The Holocaust." Men's minds are capable of the most wicked imaginations.

Swift actions of evil. It seems that man rushes to do evil, but goes slowly in doing good. The carrying out of the imaginations of his heart is swift indeed. The Nazis conquered Poland in one quick month in 1939, and within six weeks trucks were pulling up in front of Jewish homes, taking them to already prepared concentration camps for "the final solution." There is no delay in doing evil, and the feet of men run swiftly in the carrying out of it.

False Witness. The mouths of men are able to destroy reputations through a little falsehood here and an innuendo there.

Many lives have been destroyed and people driven to suicide and madness because of the false witness of others. Many others have languished in prisons or suffered degradation, poverty, and the loss of everything because of the false witness of others.

Sowing of discord. The last on the list of abominations is the person who sows discord among his brethren. Paul warned, "I beseech you, brethren, mark them which cause divisions and offenses contrary to the doctrine which ye have learned; and avoid them. For they that are such serve not our Lord Jesus Christ, but their own belly; and by good works and fair speeches deceive the hearts of the simple" (Rom. 16:17-18). It is a delight to the heart of God to see His children living together in peace and harmony: "Behold how good and how pleasant it is for brethren to dwell together in unity" (Ps. 133:1). The sin of discord and disunity comes under the special scrutiny of God. The devil works overtime to cause disharmony among the brethren. He knows the power of a united witness for Christ, for he saw it at work among believers in the Early Church.

"The multitude of them that believed were of one heart and of one soul: neither said any of them that aught of the things which he possessed was his own; but they had all things in common. And with great power gave the apostles witness of the resurrection of the Lord Jesus: and great grace was upon them all" (Acts 4:32-33).

"My son, keep thy father's commandment, and forsake not the law of thy mother: bind them continually upon thine heart, and tie them about thy neck. When thou goest, it shall lead thee; when thou sleepest, it shall keep thee; and when thou awakest, it shall talk with thee. For the commandment is a lamp, and law is light; and reproofs of instruction are the way of life" (6:20-23.)

The Word of God is our rule of faith and life. In this passage, which repeats some of the thoughts uttered earlier in the book, Solomon encourages his readers to live by that with which he governs his own life—the laws and commandments of God. This is the finest thing parents can do for their children—to lead them to the Lord and teach them to abide by the teachings of the Bible.

He explains the reason for that. The Holy Spirit can take the Word and give guidance by day, comfort by night, and refreshment for our waking moments (6:22). The best security against the encroachment of the world into our lives is to be in the Word through a daily quiet time with God.

In their pastoral prayer, ministers often pray for those who are absent from the services through sickness, indifference, travel, or other reasons. They pray that God would fan the flame of faith in the lives of those who are not there. During one of those services my mind went to our fireplace and I saw the wisdom of that kind of prayer. Often I have put wet logs on the fire, listened to them sizzle, and soon found that I had to fan the flames to keep it burning brightly. Left to itself, the log would grow smoky and dull.

Not only does the flame of faith need to be fanned, but it needs to be fed. Even the brightest fire will soon go out if more logs are not provided. In our Christian experience, the fuel for our flame of faith is the Word of God. Hence the admonition, "Bind them continually upon thine heart" (6:21).

One of the finest and most productive ways of doing this is through the consistent practice of memorizing the Word of God. As I write the Word of God on the table of my heart, the Holy Spirit feeds and nourishes my soul. My faith is fed. My spiritual life is strengthened.

Other things happen. God uses His Word to give me the guidance I need for my pilgrimage through this life. "When thou goest, it shall lead thee." This is a great promise in light of the fact that I have never before gone the road of this particular day. I do not know what it may bring forth, but I do know that God is guiding me by His Word.

David had prayed, "How precious also are Thy thoughts unto me, O God! How great is the sum of them! If I should count them, they are more in number than the sand: when I awake, I am still with Thee" (Ps. 139:17-18). This is significant in light of the words of Jesus, "Enter ye in at the strait gate: for wide is the gate, and broad is the way, that leadeth to destruction, and many there be which go in thereat: Because strait is the gate, and narrow is the way, which leadeth unto life, and few there be that find it" (Matt. 7:13-14).

Educators teach us the truth as best as they know it. Philosophers show us life as they see it. Politicians guide the affairs of men by governing through the laws of the land. But God guides us through the brilliance of the light of His Word. It is utterly reliable. It is absolute truth. It is perfectly sure. It is unchanging and eternal. If we receive the guidance of the statutes of God, our way will be clear and our path plain.

Furthermore, it is the only way we will be able to overcome the pitfalls presented to us in this chapter. This admonition is strategically located in the middle of this section to show its importance for overcoming the problems mentioned before it —debt, sloth, improper behavior, the seven deadly sins (Prov. 6:1-19)—and the deadly problem of adultery that follows this instruction (6:24-35). We can survive only by being in the Word of God.

"To keep thee from the evil woman, from the flattery of the tongue of a strange woman. Lust not after her beauty in thine own heart; neither let her take thee with her eyelids. For by means of a whorish woman a man is brought to a piece of bread: and the adulteress will hunt for the precious life. Can a man take fire in his bosom, and his clothes not be burned? Can one go upon hot coals, and his feet not be burned? So he that goeth in to his neighbor's wife; whosoever toucheth her shall not be innocent. Men do not despise a thief, if he steal to satisfy his soul when he is hungry; but if he be found, he shall restore sevenfold; he shall give all the substance of his house. But whoso committeth adultery with a woman lacketh understanding: he that doeth it destroyeth his own soul. A wound and dishonor shall he get; and his reproach shall not be wiped away. For jealousy is the rage of a man: therefore he will not spare in the day of vengeance. He will not regard any ransom; neither will he rest content, though thou givest many gifts" (6:24-35).

The temptation to the sins of the flesh, to follow the sensual appetites, is ever present and strong. We are vulnerable to the lusts of the flesh throughout most of our lives. No one is immune. Neither age nor experience of walking with God protect us from falling. Something happened when I was a young Christian that frightened me so much that it kept me awake at night. I had come to know a man who was slated to go overseas as a missionary. I was impressed with his life and testimony and was challenged by his missionary zeal.

Our church bade him farewell with the enthusiasm of a people who knew they were launching a trained Cnristian worker into the fields that were white unto harvest and needed to be reaped for the Lord. Some months passed and then word came that he had returned to America. His fellow missionaries had discovered that he was living in sin with a woman of the country to which he had gone to spread the Gospel.

I have known a number of people who have been confined to an iron lung as a result of polio before the Salk and Sabin vaccines were perfected. They have lived for years in that machine just wasting away in their bodies. I had two cousins who were in this condition for many years. I remember talking to a young man who was suffering the effects of his bout with polio. His arms and legs were skin and bones. He could not feed himself, nor even turn the pages of a book. A friend of mine asked him what was the severest hardship he found day after day.

His answer astounded me. He replied, "The temptations of the lusts of the flesh."

The dangers in this area are tremendous, for young and old alike. Let us say you were invited to visit a zoo that had its cages made of weak, rotten boards held together with small strands of string. Behind these flimsy barriers prowled powerful, ravenous animals—grizzly bears, lions, tigers, black panthers, polar bears, leopards. How would you feel about standing around in the middle of all that? Not very secure.

Inside each of us is a zoo like the one just described. It is populated by the powerful, wild, sensual drives of the human personality. Without Jesus Christ they are held in check only by those weak and frail wooden bars. The lion of lust, the various beasts of greed, envy, pride, and anger threaten to burst forth at any time. But with the Word of the Lord these cages can be strengthened.

James said, "Blessed is the man that endureth temptation: for when he is tried, he shall receive the crown of life, which the Lord hath promised to them that love Him. Let no man say when he is tempted, 'I am tempted of God;' For God cannot be tempted with evil, neither tempteth He any man. But every man is tempted, when he is drawn away of his own lust, and enticed. Then when lust hath conceived, it bringeth forth sin; and sin, when it is finished, bringeth forth death" (James 1:12-15).

Again, in the passage in Proverbs, the warning can work both ways. Although addressed to his son, Solomon could just as easily have addressed it to his daughters and reversed the pronouns used. Both sexes face the lusts of the flesh, and must be on guard constantly. It is the Word alone that can keep us from the evil persons and from the flattery they exercise. We are admonished not to lust after the beauty or handsomeness of the opposite sex, nor be taken in by any "come-on" glances (Prov. 6:24-25). Those who would lead us astray would cause us harm, and the potential cost of these entanglements is high (6:26).

Solomon then presents two vivid metaphors: holding fire against his bosom, and walking on coals (6:27-28). Our old nature is made of such flammable material that it is foolish to play with fire. We are like people walking around with half-empty gasoline drums inside of us. It is foolish to play with matches and fire when that's the case.

It is the same danger the butterfly or moth encounters when it flutters around the burning candle. Soon it will come too close and will damage its wings so that it can no longer fly.

We must guard against the immodest touch, for sin in this area is always downhill. It is foolish for us to venture close to sin, just as the moth is foolish to venture near the flame.

The summary is plain: there are no innocent parties in the sin of adultery! (6:29) And it all too often begins with a look, just as David first saw Bathsheba, then lusted, and then took her. Job had the right answer: "I made a covenant with mine eyes; why then should I think upon a maid?" (Job 31:1). The psalmist prayed, "Turn away mine eyes from beholding vanity, and quicken Thou me in Thy way" (Ps. 119:37).

To permit our eyes to feed this lust is like pouring gasoline on a bonfire; the results can be deadly. The only antidote is the Word and following the sage advice of the Apostle Paul,

"Abstain from all appearance of evil" (1 Thes. 5:22).

The solemn warning is supported by a comparison to a thief. The usual reaction to a thief, particularly one that has desperate needs, is some understanding but with the demand of restitution. But adultery leads to spiritual destruction and social suicide.

In this passage we learn of the predictable reactions to thievery and adultery. The man who steals a loaf of bread to keep from starving or to feed a hungry family is looked on with some sympathy (6:30). He will have to repay, yes, but he is not disgraced and thrown out of his society (6:31). But not so with the man who steals his neighbor's wife. This man receives no pity; he is looked on with scorn. He was not feeding his hunger, but satisfying his lust. He was not in want, but was merely wanton.

The strong language used by Solomon in this section is repeated by the Apostle Paul. "But fornication, and all uncleanness, or covetousness, let it not be once named among you, as becometh saints; neither filthiness, nor foolish talking, nor jesting, which are not convenient: but rather giving of thanks. For this ye know, that no whoremonger, nor unclean person, nor covetous man, who is an idolater, hath any inheritance in the kingdom of Christ and of God. Let no man deceive you with vain words: for because of these things cometh the wrath of God upon the children of disobedience. Be not ye therefore partakers with them" (Eph. 5:3-7).

Often the adulterer cannot even forgive himself. After the disastrous deed is done and he regains his senses, he looks on himself with unforgiving hatred. He despises himself for bringing shame on his name for a moment of illicit pleasure. His delight of the moment has turned to torment, and it continues day and night. "A wound and dishonor shall he get, and his reproach shall not be wiped away" (Prov. 6:33).

He has incurred the rage of his neighbor that may lead to violence and vengeance. We need to watch and pray that God will protect us from this awful sin. "Wherefore let him that thinketh he standeth take heed lest he fall" (1 Cor. 10:12).

10

Wisdom's Parable on Chastity

Proverbs 7:1-27

Because of the importance of this subject of godly living for the children of God, Solomon continues his warnings and instruction concerning immorality and chastity. The argument of this section resembles the one just preceding it (6:20-35), but is presented this time in the form of a drama.

The introduction (7:1-5) again presents the means by which this temptation can be resisted—the Word of God. Similar language to that used previously in the book is given to protect the child of God from temptation to immorality and uncleanness.

The drama (7:6-23) portrays the simple youth who goes out into the night ill prepared to meet the temptations of the alluring harlot, who seduces him and lures him to his destruction.

The conclusion (7:24-27) applies this episode to the lives of the readers and listeners by giving a defense against falling into this sin.

"My son, keep my words, and lay up my commandments with thee. Keep my commandments, and live; and my law as the apple of thine eye. Bind them upon thy fingers, write them upon the table of thine heart. Say unto wisdom, 'Thou art my sister;' and call understanding thy kinswoman; that they may keep thee

from the strange woman, from the stranger which flattereth with her words" (7:1-5).

Solomon again speaks to us in the name of the Lord and encourages us to obey and apply Scripture to our lives. As we have looked at this book, a fascinating truth has confronted us time and again. He has commended us to the Word of God with an earnest appeal to keep it, live by it, and trust it totally.

Now if Solomon were an ordinary man who was a follower of God, that fact might not be too noticeable. But he is known to be the wisest of men, and he is imploring us to listen not to *him* but to *God*. Admittedly he does share with us the wisdom he has received from the Lord, but on many occasions he simply turns us to the Scriptures themselves.

He describes the Word of God as a treasure to be kept secure. When a person has something of great value, he treats it with care. If he doesn't, he may live to regret it. An expensive camera I had bought in Hong Kong was stolen from my hotel room while I was in Dallas. I had left it carelessly on the chest of drawers, and when I returned later that day it was gone. I had not treated it with care.

The devil is out to rob us of the effects of the Word of God in our lives. "And these are they by the wayside, where the Word is sown; but when they have heard, Satan cometh immediately, and taketh away the Word that was sown in their hearts" (Mark 4:15). He can rob us of the influence of the Word by causing us to doubt it, disobey it, or disregard it.

Solomon's admonition is strong. We must keep the Word of God as something without which we simply cannot live. In our physical diet, certain things are "musts" without which we grow weak and sickly. I spoke with a missionary who told of the ill effects on him when the diet of the country in which he was serving did not provide him with enough iron. A friend of mine in the Middle East suffered ill effects because of the lack of Vitamin B. We need daily supplies of certain ingredients for our bodies' well-being. So it is with the Word of God. Jesus taught, "Man shall not live by bread alone, but by every word that proceedeth out of the mouth of God" (Matt. 4:4).

In light of all this, is it any wonder that God's command is for us to write the Word of God on the tables of our hearts?

This is a positive practice that has blessed the hearts of millions, and these, in turn, have been used of God to bless the lives of countless others. The Word of God must be central in our lives, the very apple—the most important thing—of our eyes.

A few months ago, I needed some answers on the subject of forgiveness. I wrote to Dr. Jack Mitchell at Multnomah School of the Bible in Portland, Oregon, and asked if he could send me some thoughts on that subject. He sent me a tape in which he shared some Scriptures about the topic. I was again amazed at this man's command of the Bible. Scores of passages flowed from his lips as he discussed the issue. People travel from far and wide to hear this man speak—not because of his innate wisdom but because he has, over the years, faithfully written the Word of God on the table of his heart.

Do this and you too will live the promised abundant life, and your life will become a blessing to others around you who may have great needs.

Solomon then gives two more words of advice on the subject of wisdom in its keeping power from temptation to immorality. This also is a recurring subject in the Book of Proverbs and for a good reason. True wisdom on *any* subject is hard to find. When a man is an authority on a subject, the world beats a path to his door. Students often choose a university because they want to study under an expert in the field of their chosen study. They pick a seminary or medical school on the same basis. They want to be exposed to the wisdom of that professor or scholar in order that they, in turn, will be more useful to the world in their field.

First, Solomon encourages us to an intimate acquaintance with godly wisdom, the kind of intimate knowledge that we have with a brother or sister. Two children who grow up together really know each other. The fondness between them is often deep and lasting.

When our daughter, Becky, was married, our younger son felt her departure deeply. We had taken a trip to the East Coast immediately after the wedding, and on returning home Randy asked that we keep the door closed to what had been Becky's room. He said, "When it's closed, I can pretend she's still there." They had their squabbles like any brother and sister, but in the final analysis there was a very deep love there.

This is the relationship to wisdom that Solomon encourages all of us to have. "Say unto wisdom, 'Thou art my sister!'" Wisdom, doing things God's way, is to be something we dearly love and in which we take great delight. If we mentally review the positive effects of wisdom in our lives and the dangers that ignorance or going our own way brings, we should understand the reason for Solomon's repetition of this command.

Second, Solomon mentions that wisdom is a strong defense. This may be seen in every area of life. If I am aware of the fact that there are mosquitoes around that carry malaria, I will sleep under a mosquito net. If I know there are sharks in the water, I will swim near the shore with extreme caution. If there are thieves in the neighborhood, I will keep my doors locked at night. If a local merchant is a crook, I will make my purchases elsewhere. My wisdom in these matters is my defense.

Here the defense is against the strange woman who flatters with her words. (It could also be the strange man who lures a young girl into immorality with his sweet words.) He warns against her. If we know where acquaintance with her will lead, we will avoid her at all costs. To be forewarned is to be forearmed.

Two kinds of defense are possible. One is a good, positive offense that leads us to avoid all this by being engaged in that which is good and wholesome. The other is to avoid the unnecessary contact that is prompted by temptation dumped on us daily by the world—the entertainment field, the literature of the day, and unwholesome companions. Wisdom will lead us aright.

"For at the window of my house I looked through my casement, and beheld among the simple ones, I discerned among the youths, a young man void of understanding, passing through the street near her corner; and he went the way to her house, in the twilight, in the evening, in the black and dark night: And, behold, there met him a woman with the attire of an harlot, and subtil of heart. (She is loud and stubborn; her feet abide not in her house: now is she without, now in the streets, and lieth in wait at every corner.) So she caught him, and kissed him, and with an impudent face said unto him, 'I have peace offerings

with me; this day have I payed my vows. Therefore came I forth to meet thee, diligently to seek thy face, and I have found thee. I have decked my bed with coverings of tapestry, with carved works, with fine linen of Egypt. I have perfumed my bed with myrrh, aloes, and cinnamon. Come, let us take our fill of love until the morning; let us solace ourselves with loves. For the goodman is not at home, he is gone a long journey: he hath taken a bag of money with him, and will come home at the day appointed.' With her much fair speech she caused him to yield, with the flattering of her lips she forced him. He goeth after her straightway, as an ox goeth to the slaughter, or as a fool to the correction of the stocks; till a dart strike through his liver; as a bird hasteth to the snare, and knoweth not that it is for his life." (7:6-23).

The tragic drama with which Solomon confronts us here is an old story that is repeated many times today. As young man is ensnared by a wicked woman. (A young girl is enticed by a wicked man; an older man or woman is lured into this sin.)

Geoff, a friend of mine in the Air Force, was flying overseas to his new assignment. On the plane he met another man who was a member of a good, Bible-believing church in America, who expressed interest in doing some Bible study when they located on their new base. Geoff was delighted, and told him he would come by his motel room next morning to have some fellowship and prayer.

That morning Geoff went to this man's motel, found the room, and walked in. The man was there with one of the local prostitutes. He hadn't lasted 24 hours before falling prey to the wiles of a wicked woman.

If this tragic story which Solomon so dramatically recounted were staged by our film industry and made into a motion picture, it would probably not be a tragedy. The harlot would probably be the star of the show. The audience would be regaled with laughter as she tricked the young country bumpkin into her snare. Her evil ways would be trumpeted as a victory for a life-style of fun and frolic, the carrying out of the new morality and freedom of the modern age.

But this passage is no comedy. It is a sad tale of the destruction and ruin of a young man. The parts of the story are: the unprepared victim (7:6-9), the seductive woman (7:10-12), her approach and devices (7:13-21), and the victim's fall (7:22-23).

The unprepared victim. Here is a young man out on the sea of life with no pilot to guide him or compass to chart his course. He has not called wisdom his sister nor understanding his kinswoman. He is not taking in the Word of God; he is "void of understanding" because he does not have the Scripture to lead him in his ways. He walks through life daily and nightly in the midst of sensual temptations that are constantly around.

He has probably chosen the company of other young fools. Had he chosen a better crowd to run with, there might have been some hope for him. Solomon, later in this book, warns, "He that walketh with wise men shall be wise: but a companion of fools shall be destroyed" (13:20).

He made another fatal mistake, one repeated so many times today. He had nothing to do. He had too much leisure time on his hands. He was just passing through the street, going nowhere, doing nothing. Had he been engaged in some worthwhile sport or other positive activity, he might have been spared. But he was walking about in a tough part of town at night with nothing to do. He was asking for trouble, and he got it.

The seductive woman. She must have seen him coming, so she went out to meet him. This is the way of the woman of the streets from antiquity. The description fits the situation in any city in the world—Yokosuka, Japan or Colorado Springs, Colorado.

Outwardly she must have been very appealing, dressed "fit to kill," if you please. But inwardly she was "loud and stubborn," Solomon tells us parenthetically. She was a woman who could not stay home, but had to be out in the streets lying in wait for the unwary. It would certainly be an unequal contest.

Her approach and devices. Impudently she catches her victim and kisses him right there in the street. Then she tells him of the occasion—it's a special day—and invites him to help her celebrate. She lures him further by telling him that she has sought *him* out and thus bolsters his ego. She beguiles his mind with a sensual description of her bedroom and invites him to join her on the bed of "love." She assures him that her husband is out of town and that he has nothing to fear. The whole approach is pressed home with many flattering words.

The victim's fall. Unprepared as he was, there was no hope for him. So he went, a dumb ox to the slaughter. He went to his ruin totally oblivious to the dangers involved. Quite possibly he went laughing to his doom. His foolish mind had visions of sensual pleasures and what he saw in the offing was good times and great fun with a beautiful woman. All this was in his thoughts as he went headlong to destruction. Just like a bird going to its death in a carefully placed snare.

The Apostle John said, concerning this kind of behavior, "We know that whosoever is born of God sinneth not [does not practice sin continuously]; but he that is begotten of God keepeth himself, and that wicked one toucheth him not" (1 John 5:18).

We have the solemn responsibility to use the wisdom that God has given us through His Word. We have the responsibility to follow the directions of Scripture. Ours is the responsibility to keep ourselves from the company of fools, from the environment of evil that will lead to shame, sorrow, sickness, and a hardening of our hearts toward God. It is a warning that is so vitally needed in our day when we are surrounded on all sides by pornography, lewdness, and the call to the new morality.

"Hearken unto me now therefore, O ye children, and attend to the words of my mouth. Let not thine heart decline to her ways, go not astray in her paths. For she hath cast down many wounded: yea, many strong men have been slain by her. Her house is the way to hell, going down to the chambers of death" (7:24-27).

What would your response be to the following situation? You live near a hospital in a certain town. Day after day you observe a strange and terrible sight. Near where you live is a broad street, and each day thousands of people head down that street, and every evening many of them are carried back and into the hospital wounded, broken, and bloody. Those who go that way on the broad street are perfectly aware that in all likelihood they will be carried back that night in the same dreadful condition. Yet they still clamor on, pushing forward, insisting on heading in the direction that leads to destruction.

Wouldn't you wonder about such strange behavior? Wouldn't you think they would eventually see the folly of going that way? Wouldn't you think that street would soon be deserted and empty of all traffic? But that is not the way of the world. The street remains jammed with people, shoving their way along in the crowd, only to be brought back later in a desperate and critical condition.

That is the situation Solomon is trying to prevent with this conclusion to his drama, his parable on chastity. He is trying to cut the youth off at the pass and save him from the heartache and agony that comes to those who choose the path of sin. He urges him along the straight and narrow path that leads to life in all its fullness. He cautions him to keep his heart from inching in the wrong direction. He pleads with him to refrain his feet from the path of sensual appetites and the lust of the flesh.

Note the words and phrases that appear in describing the seducing power of the strange woman: decline her ways, don't stray into her paths, she wounds many, she slays strong men, the way to her is the way to hell, her rooms are the very chambers of death. Here is an ominous picture, a description of sorrow, destruction, and degradation. Isn't it amazing how the devil can take that picture and make it appear good, attractive, desirable, and something to be sought eagerly? It baffles many godly Christians how something so rotten and foul, so destructive and dangerous, can be made so alluring and so appealing.

This path downward often begins with an impure thought triggered by a book or magazine, a TV program or movie, a filthy conversation, or a lewd joke. If you learn to stop at that first step, you can avoid the path altogether. If you allow yourself to play with that initial temptation, you may soon find yourself on a slippery way in which there is no turning back.

The Christian must heed strongly Paul's warning to the Colossians: "If ye then be risen with Christ, seek those things which are above, where Christ sitteth on the right hand of God. Set your affections on things above, not on things of the earth. . . . Mortify therefore your members which are upon the earth; fornication, uncleanness, inordinate affection, evil concupiscence, and covetousness, which is idolatry: for which things' sake the wrath of God cometh on the children of disobedience" (Col. 3:1-2, 5-6).

Peter's words still ring true today: "Dearly beloved, I beseech you as strangers and pilgrims, abstain from fleshly lusts, which war against the soul" (1 Peter 2:11). Shame and disgrace await those who ignore these words.

11

In Praise
of Wisdom

Proverbs 8:1-36

Throughout the Book of Proverbs Solomon has been discussing wisdom. At times he has personified her (wisdom is always mentioned in the feminine), and had her speak through him. Since wisdom is the heart and soul of this book and his teaching in it, she has been an important subject of discussion, warning, and instruction.

We come now to the high point of the first part of this book in two chapters that both personify wisdom and ascribe to her the praise that is due her. The passage is one of great beauty, and some commentators see in it a preincarnate manifestation of the Lord Jesus Christ in the role of wisdom, particularly in the section on Creation (Prov. 8:22-31). The point of the whole is not so much to impress the reader with a glorious description of wisdom as it is to motivate him to certain godly actions. The thrust of the passage is to stir the Christian to apply the Word of God to his own life so that he can go through life following the path God has set before him. The essence of man's response to wisdom is simply living according to God's plan—being and doing what God wants us to be and do.

The section divides into five parts: wisdom as a guide (8:1-5); wisdom as a way of life (8:6-13); the rewards wisdom brings (8:14-21); wisdom and creation (8:22-31); and the necessary response to wisdom (8:32-36).

"Doth not wisdom cry? And understanding put forth her voice? She standeth in the top of high places, by the way in the places of the paths. She crieth at the gates, at the entry of the city, at the coming in at the doors. 'Unto you, O men, I call; and my voice is to the sons of man. O ye simple, understand wisdom: and, ye fools, be ye of an understanding heart' " (8:1-5).

At first I did not know where the voice was coming from. I was standing on a busy street in downtown Paris, and I could hear someone calling in a low, husky whisper. I turned and saw a man approaching me from the shadows of a narrow alley. He was well-dressed, about 45 years old, glancing from side to side.

He moved in close to me and whispered, "Hey, Monsieur, you want to buy some dirty pictures?"

When I told him I had no use for them, he politely backed off and went scurrying down the boulevard. He seemed to be operating under the cloak of respectability, but was doing his best to avoid the eyes of the gendarmes.

The ways of God are in stark contrast to the ways of men when they peddle their smut. Men often do it in secret. Here wisdom cries not in secret, but openly on top of the high places, in the crowded streets, at the gates of the city, everywhere where people gather (8:2-3). In contrast to the hidden and darkened ways of sin under the shadow of night, wisdom is calling in the marketplace where the truth might be heard and believed by all who are there.

The message is plain. The truth is stated fearlessly and without hesitation. Isaiah taught, "Behold, the Lord's hand is not shortened, that it cannot save; neither His ear heavy, that it cannot hear: but your iniquities have separated between you and your God, and your sins have hid His face from you, that He will not hear. For your hands are defiled with blood, and your fingers with iniquity; your lips have spoken lies, your tongue hath muttered perverseness. None calleth for justice, nor any pleadeth for truth: they trust in vanity, and speak lies; they conceive mischief, and bring forth iniquity. . . . Their feet run to evil, and they make haste to shed innocent blood: their thoughts are thoughts of iniquity; wasting and destruction are in their paths. The way of peace they know not; and there is no judgment in their goings: they have made them crooked paths: whosoever goeth therein shall not know peace" (Isa. 59:1-4, 7-8).

Both testaments ring with the message of forgiveness, salvation, and hope. "The Lord is not slack concerning His promise, as some men count slackness; but is longsuffering to us-ward, not willing that any should perish, but that all should come to repentance" (2 Peter 3:9).

Toward the end of His ministry, Jesus answered the high priest about His teachings and what He stood for: "I spake openly to the world; I ever taught in the synagogue, and in the temple, whither the Jews always resort; and in secret have I said nothing. Why askest thou Me? Ask them which heard Me, what I have said unto them: behold, they know what I said" (John 18:20-21).

Jesus Christ is the embodiment of wisdom and truth. This is an all-important fact to remember when we realize that a message based on falsehood, lies, superstition, and error is deadly and of no value at all. At the same time, a message based on truth does little good if no one hears it.

Ignorance is a terrible thing. Because of it diseases spread; because of it lives that could be full and productive are shallow and wasted; because of it whole societies live in fear and engage in the most abominable and outlandish practices. Every night at the same hour a young woman in the heart of Africa is wracked with dreadful pain. Her mother, a witch doctor, has put a curse on her, and now in addition to the nightly spasms of pain that grip her body, strange and horrible voices call to her in the night.

Again this year, in a wild and awesome festival thousands of people in Asia will pierce their flesh with hooks and drive skewers through ther cheeks and tongues to honor their gods.

In another remote area of the world, a little six-year-old girl was saved from death at the hands of the elders of her tribe. She had been judged responsible for the drought that had ravaged the area. Her grandfather had contacted the missionaries who agreed to take the little orphan to a place of safety.

In the center of the African continent is a fierce and blood-thirsty tribe which frequently raids its neighbors. These people are merciless warriors who attack women, children, and old people and strew their intestines on nearby trees and bushes. They live where life is hard; they supplement their diet with blood drunk from the open vein in the neck of a cow. Hatred and anger motivate their daily lives.

Today there is another society where women wear huge metal bracelets that are permanently fastened to their bodies. These are heavy, awkward things, and the women are required to wear 11 of them on each of their arms and legs and three around their necks. Some women carry as much as 100 pounds of metal on their bodies day and night.

Today there is still another society where an unwanted or cursed child may be destroyed by crushing its head or strangling it at birth. No one cares. Ignorance and darkness are the orders of the day.

But today is also a day when selfless, humble, and highly motivated missionaries of the Christian Gospel have taken the message of Jesus Christ and the wisdom of God to a world that is helpless and hopeless without it. They have gone to dispel the darkness and ignorance with the light and truth of the Gospel of Jesus Christ who is the very wisdom of God. They treat the sick, educate the unlearned, train able minds, and bring salvation to the souls of many. Often they have little or no privacy, sleep on camp cots or worse, and contend with muddy water, heat, dust, flies, mosquitoes, and snakes. Some die from local diseases, and others are shot, beheaded, or beaten to death. Yet they and many others go on, proclaiming the Good News from the top of the high places, in the places of the paths, and in the gates of the cities.

Today Christian businessmen are sharing the Gospel in the marketplaces of the world; today Christian doctors and nurses are sharing the Gospel with the sick and dying. Today Christian men in our state and federal governments are sharing the Gospel in the public buildings of our land; today Christian college students are sharing the Gospel on university campuses. Today Christian servicemen are sharing the Gospel with their fellow soldiers, sailors, airmen, and marines. Today house-wives are sharing the Gospel in their neighborhoods; today high school students are sharing the Gospel with their class-mates.

Businessmen's luncheons, prayer breakfasts, campus out-reach, neighborhood coffee Bible studies, high school Bible clubs, and servicemen's centers are all being used of God to spread the message of Jesus Christ openly, "This is the way, walk ye in it" (Isa. 30:21). It is all out in the open. The voice of wisdom cries openly to all men.

"Hear, for I will speak of excellent things; and the opening of my lips shall be right things. For my mouth shall speak truth; and wickedness is an abomination to my lips. All the words of my mouth are in righteousness; there is nothing froward or perverse in them. They are all plain to him that understandeth, and right to them that find knowledge. Receive my instruction, and not silver; and knowledge rather than choice gold. For wisdom is better than rubies; and all the things that may be desired are not to be compared to it. I wisdom dwell with pru-dence, and find out knowledge of witty inventions. The fear of the Lord is to hate evil: pride, and arrogancy, and the evil way, the froward mouth, do I hate" (8:6-13).

The way of wisdom is the way of excellence. Since the ways of God are revealed clearly and are always out in the open, that which they offer is right, true, righteous, and plain. Wickedness, frowardness, and perversion are totally alien to Him. This means that when a man takes God's wisdom as his own way of life, it will be characterized by that which is wholesome and good. This is what Jesus promised, when He said that He had come to give men life and that more abundantly (John 10:10).

This passage expounds the *rightness* of wisdom as a way of life; it contrasts so starkly with the life of wickedness as shown elsewhere in the Book of Proverbs! And those who had found the true way of life testify to the difference between them. John Newton, the slaver, became the great Christian hymn-writer. Charles Colson, the hatchetman for the Watergate con-spiracy, became the compassionate worker with men in prison. Eldridge Cleaver, the Black Panther revolutionary, became the lucid spokesman for the evangelical faith. To those who under-stand and have found knowledge, the way is plain (8:9).

Solomon compares wisdom to valuable material things, such as silver, gold, and rubies, but there really is no comparison. Wisdom is far more valuable than all the silver, gold, and precious stones in the world. To have wisdom is to have life, not material things that will eventually perish. Nothing in this world can compare with it.

Wisdom, furthermore, "dwells with prudence." If a person is ice-skating on a lake and sees a sign stating, "Danger! Thin Ice!" the prudent thing to do is obvious—skate somewhere else. If a person is approaching a house that has a large sign saying, "Beware of Dog!" the prudent thing is to proceed with caution. When an epidemic of measles broke out in a high school in my hometown, people prudently lined up for innoculations.

These are examples of one definition of the word *prudent*. It means to exercise discretion and caution. When I first read this verse (8:12), I assumed that to be the meaning of the word. Imagine my surprise to discover it to be a word that is usually used in a bad or negative sense.

The word here means smoothness, cunning, craftiness, and subtlety. That doesn't mean these are the attributes of wisdom. The wisdom of God is not that at all. The Bible refers to the devil as the subtle one (see Gen. 3:1); trickery and deceit are his stock-in-trade.

The way of the Lord is just the opposite. He always tells the truth just as it is. Some might believe that this approach puts God at a disadvantage, that subtlety and cleverness would have the edge over plain straightforwardness. But that is not so. The wisdom of God lives with that kind of stuff and reveals its falsehood to all (8:12).

No matter how subtle or clever, no matter how smooth and cunning, when the light of the wisdom of God is revealed, the truth is brought to light, and error and deceit are exposed for what they are.

Jesus Christ stated in no uncertain terms that He was the Truth (John 14:6). The Apostle John tells us that Jesus came to destroy the works of the devil (1 John 3:8). Put those two thoughts together and we see this remarkable fact: by His entrance into the world as Truth, by living the truth, by His straightforward openness, Jesus met the devil head-on and defeated him.

This is the great lesson to us. In a less than perfect world filled with clever people, many of whom are committed to a life-style contrary to Scripture, the wisest thing we can do is to stay on the path of truth that Jesus showed us. At times it may not appear to be "hep" or "cool." Young men and women at the airports in saffron robes, or distributing carnations in neat western attire, may exhort you to follow a new and exotic voice from Asia. Drug pushers may paint a rosy picture of an exciting life just around the corner. But remember, Jesus said, "I am come that [you] may have life and . . . have it more abundantly" (John 10:10).

The final thing Solomon teaches here is that it is the nature of God to hate evil. The wrath of God is against everything that militates against the welfare of His children. The doctor in the jungle does his best to destroy the root causes of diseases that cripple and kill his patients. The teacher in the mission school does everything in his power to eliminate the causes of ignorance and poverty among his students. So it is with God. He sets His power and grace against all those things that would destroy our souls.

But the other side of the truth is equally important. It is impossible to hate evil unless we love that which is good. Unless that fact is brought to the forefront of our lives, we can go through our days manifesting a cranky, bitter, grouchy spirit. It is not enough just to be *against* evil; we must also be *for* that which is good.

To do that we must keep our eyes open to the total scope of life. A park in our town is frequented by people bent on immorality. Some push drugs; their language is foul and their conversation lewd. It would be easy to look at them and assume that our young people are lost to the service of the devil. But one should visit some of our churches today and by contrast see the greatest gang of turned-on kids leading Bible studies, witnessing for Christ, teaching the children, and serving the Saviour in dozens of ways.

To catch the impact of this last verse (v. 13), we must realize that God is not about to declare a truce with the devil. The kingdom of heaven is dead set against the evils of hell.

Four things in this statement call for the wrath of God. *Pride* is at the top of the list. Here is one of those sins that crops up at the most unexpected times. Something happens that I do not like, and I bristle. I raise my voice; I demand my rights. Later, when things settle down, I have to get before the Lord, ask His forgiveness, and confess my sin. Pride is a sin that God hates.

The second is *arrogance*. It is a contradiction of terms for a disciple of the one who made Himself of no reputation, who calls on us to learn of Him, the meek and lowly one, to strut about the earth bloated with a haughty spirit.

Next is the *evil* way. As we follow the Shepherd of our souls, He will lead us in the paths of righteousness for His name's sake. Godliness is a trademark of the true disciple.

The last on the list is the *froward mouth*. It is easy to look into the heart of man. Just listen to what comes out of his mouth. It is a dead giveaway. But the heart filled with Jesus Christ loves to sing praises to God.

All of us need to check this list carefully so that the Spirit of God might note the flaws in our lives and graciously deal with them. Wisdom calls on us to follow its way of life.

"Counsel is mine, and sound wisdom: I am understanding; I have strength. By Me kings reign, and princes decree justice. By Me princes rule, and nobles, even all the judges of the earth. I love them that love Me, and those that seek Me early shall find Me. Riches and honor are with Me; yea, durable riches and righteousness. My fruit is better than gold, yea, than fine gold; and My revenue than choice silver. I lead in the way of righteousness, in the midst of the paths of judgment: that I may cause those that love Me to inherit substance; and I will fill their treasures" (8:14-21).

Wisdom brings many rewards, both spiritual and material. Among these is counsel that is sound and understanding that is strong.

I was speaking at a conference in Tucson, Arizona where I met a brilliant young scientist from Lebanon. He had degrees from our finest universities, was highly respected by his peers, and was working with our government in national security matters. While we were together, he shared with me his concern for the spiritual welfare of the thousands of Lebanese who had fled their homeland and had settled in the United States.

He was wondering whether he should leave his prestigious, secure, well-paying job and get into something which would give him more time to share the Word of God with his people. It was a big decision with all kinds of social and financial implications.

But here was the fascinating thing. He was not trying to reason things out; he was praying things through. We prayed together about this matter, and left it with the Lord, trusting Him to reveal His counsel and wisdom.

That is what counsel is all about. God's counsel is based on sound wisdom and is therefore absolutely trustworthy. It is the height of foolishness to turn to the wisdom of the world for our guidance. God is eager to reveal His exciting, unpredictable, adventuresome way to us. The world is so stilted; the ways of God are so grand.

Note carefully the wording of this opening verse. The Lord does not just *have* understanding, He *is* understanding. It is the essence of His nature. And then He speaks of His strength. This has two applications. God has the strength to carry out His plans, for He is the Lord God Almighty. Second, if we rest in Him and admit our weaknesses, His strength is available to us. He perfects His strength in our weaknesses.

As followers of Jesus Christ we have all the resources of God available to us. "The Spirit of the Lord shall rest upon Him, the Spirit of wisdom and understanding, the Spirit of counsel and might, the Spirit of knowledge and of the fear of the Lord" (Isa. 11:2).

Another reward that wisdom brings to God's people is the assurance that He is in control. I once spoke with a young marine who was afraid that Marine Corps would transfer him from his present job and put him into something he would not like. He enjoyed what he was doing and did not want a change.

After he had shared the whole story with me, I began asking him some questions. Was it just his physical comfort he was thinking about? No, it wasn't. He was leading a Bible study on that base, and the Lord was using it in the lives of a number of other men. Some had already received Christ as their personal Saviour and Lord, and were growing and developing in their new lives. Others were right on the verge of becoming Christians. He knew that if he left, the ministry might come to a standstill. He wanted it to continue, and was praying for his unsaved friends and young believers.

I asked another question. Who was in charge of his orders? He wasn't sure, but guessed it was some officer in the personnel office. I told him he was wrong with his guess.

"OK," he said, "probably someone who runs the personnel computer, the officer responsible for the transfer of men and filling jobs that are vacant." Wrong again.

"Was it my first sergeant?" No.

"Was it the commandant of the Marine Corps?" Still wrong.

"OK, then, who was it?"

I told him it was God. As a Christian he was under the direct, personal control of a loving heavenly Father who was guiding and guarding everything that happened to him. If God wanted to work through a personnel officer or even the commandant, He could do it.

No earthly power can thwart God's plans for His own. "All the inhabitants of the earth are reputed as nothing: and He doeth according to His will in the army of heaven, and among the inhabitants of the earth: and none can stay His hand, or say unto Him, 'What doest Thou?' " (Dan. 4:35)

God is in complete control, "The Lord reigneth; let the earth rejoice; let the multitude of isles be glad thereof. . . . Ye that love the Lord, hate evil: He preserveth the souls of His saints; He delivereth them out of the hand of the wicked" (Ps. 97:1, 10).

It is amazing how many Christians have a hang-up about God's ability to control our lives. I spoke with a college student at the University of Pittsburgh one day, and he told me he had figured out his schedule just the way he wanted it. When he showed it to his advisor, he had to change it because some of the classes were full. This upset him terribly.

Businessmen are transferred by their companies and they worry and fret. Somehow they are not really convinced of these words: "By Me kings reign, and princes decree justice. By Me princes rule, and nobles, even all the judges of the earth" (Prov. 8:15-16). God knows each of our situations and is in control of all things.

Another reward of wisdom is that we can apprehend the love

of God consciously and claim the promise of His presence with us daily.

It is a fascinating thing to realize that one of the last questions Jesus asked one of His disciples was, "Peter, do you love Me?" Three times He asked it, "Do you love Me?"

After all the training Peter had received. After all the time Peter had spent with Jesus. After all the experiences they had gone through together. Together on the raging sea in a sinking boat; together as the 5,000 were fed with a few loaves and fishes; together as the dead were raised, the blind received sight, the deaf were given hearing, the lame walked, and the lepers were cleansed; together in the Upper Room. After all that, the question still came, "Do you love Me?"

No one loves God as a result of his natural inclinations, "because the carnal mind is enmity against God, for it is not subject to the law of God, neither indeed can be" (Rom. 8:7).

But God in His grace infuses our spirits with His Spirit and the fruit of the Spirit is love. He lights the fire of life in us, and "we love Him, because He first loved us" (1 John 4:19).

The verse then speaks of those who love and seek God. Here again if there is the slightest inclination to seek God with our whole hearts, it does not come from within us but from heaven above. God in His grace plants the desire in our hearts.

When God inclines our hearts to seek Him—especially in our daily devotional life with Him—we are given one of the great and precious promises of the Bible. If we seek, we will find Him. Jesus stated, "Ask, and it shall be given you; seek, and ye shall find; knock, and it shall be opened unto you: For everyone that asketh receiveth; and he that seeketh findeth; and to him that knocketh it shall be opened" (Matt. 7:7-8).

The testimony of David is a beautiful and simple guide for us to follow: "O God, Thou art my God; early will I seek Thee: my soul thirsteth for Thee, my flesh longeth for Thee in a dry and thirsty land, where no water is" (Ps. 63:1). The most practical thing we can do in our daily lives is to seek the Lord early each morning.

The last of the benefits of wisdom presented in this passage is that of wealth and riches, predominantly spiritual but also a hint of the material.

Whenever we visit someone in the hospital, my wife takes

along some flowers. She never takes a bouquet, but always a potted plant. Cut flowers soon fade; they may be nice to look at, but they are already in the process of rapid decay. The potted plant may not look quite as nice, but it will last. The patient can take it home and with proper care can enjoy it for months or years to come.

Solomon states that wisdom has with it *durable* riches (8:18). This is a rare word that can be translated "enduring," which gives the idea of ancient, that which has been around for a long time and therefore will last for a long while as well.

In a day of high prices and ongoing inflation, that is an important fact to consider. It is important for us to spend our hard-earned money on something that will last. So we shop for a sofa that has a durable cover; we shop for tires that will last for at least 40,000 miles; we look for shoes with sturdy soles; we search for appliances that have good warranties.

Here the Lord is offering riches, honor, and the righteousness that will not tarnish, fade, or decay. What He offers, of course, are the unsearchable riches of Christ. He offers the honor of being a bondslave to the Saviour. He offers to clothe us in the righteousness of the Son of God.

In contrast, the devil comes to us with an entirely different proposition. His riches are the glitter and glamor of the world. His honor is the prestige of worldly power. His righteousness comes by self-effort. This can take the form of any of a hundred man-made religions; it can take the form of deeds that call attention to ourselves and that put us on a pedestal in the eyes of others.

But Jesus taught, "Lay not up for yourselves treasures upon earth, where moth and rust doth corrupt, and where thieves break through and steal: But lay up for yourselves treasures in heaven, where neither moth nor rust doth corrupt, and where thieves do not break through nor steal: For where your treasure is, there will your heart be also" (Matt. 6:19-21).

In light of this, it doesn't seem that it would be hard to choose the way of God and wisdom over the ways of the world. But it is, for the temporal has an attraction that is all too real. It appeals to our human natures, to our pride. But the spiritual riches are so much more satisfying than all that the world can offer, for we truly inherit His substance, and our spiritual treasure houses will be full. Wisdom brings with it its high rewards.

"The Lord possessed me in the beginning of His way, before His works of old. I was set up from everlasting, from the beginning, or ever the earth was. When there were no depths, I was brought forth; when there were no fountains abounding with water. Before the mountains were settled, before the hills was I brought forth: while as yet He had not made the earth, nor the fields, nor the highest part of the dust of the world. When He prepared the heavens, I was there: when He set a compass upon the face of the depth: when He established the clouds above: when He strengthened the fountains of the deep: when He gave to the sea His decree, that the waters should not pass His commandment: when He appointed the foundations of the earth: then I was by Him, as one brought up with Him: and I was daily His delight, rejoicing always before Him; rejoicing in the habitable part of His earth; and my delights were with the sons of men" (8:22-31).

Before I became a Christian I was confronted with the fact that Jesus Christ did not begin His life in the manger of Bethlehem. As I read the New Testament and studied other passages, I saw that Jesus was the eternal Christ, the Son of the living God. He was "in the beginning;" He was with the Father "before the world was."

As the years passed following my conversion, I recall wondering what Jesus had been doing all that "time." Was He designing the architecture of the world? Was He planning the redemption of mankind? Was He enjoying the fellowship of the Father or the adoration of the angels? What *was* He doing?

In this passage we are given a glimpse behind the curtains of eternity. We are thrust back beyond the ages and taken directly into the council halls of time "before the world was." Here we see the embodiment of the wisdom of God—the Lord Jesus Christ, the Lord of glory. In His grace and goodness, He hands us a signed self-portrait. We see Him as the everlasting Son of God, in whom the Father was eternally pleased to dwell. He is the elect of God who brought daily delight to the Father (Isa. 42:1). At the time of the transfiguration of Jesus, the Father spoke these words, "This is My beloved Son, in whom I am well pleased" (Matt. 17:5).

But we are also confronted by a strange and wonderful thing. We see Jesus rejoicing, not only before the Father, but in His own words, "My delights were with the sons of men" (8:31). Man who rebelled so horribly against the love of God; man who had been created in the image of God but chose to follow the temptations of the devil; man who was to nail the Son of God to a cross, to crown Him with thorns; man who was to beat Him up so badly that His visage was marred more than any other man who was the object of His love and delight.

Who can begin to fathom the depths of that truth? Who can explain that? Thank God we are not called on to explain it but to rejoice in it. Jesus voluntarily left His throne of glory and the adoration of heaven for the scorn of this world.

I was on a flight from Washington, D.C. to Los Angeles when the pilot announced over the intercom that the Grand Canyon could be seen on the right side of the plane. It was a cloudless day and we were flying at 39,000 feet. I looked out and was awestruck by the sight. There in its majesty and splendor was one of the most beautiful sights in the world. Its tremendous size, its brilliant colors, its depth, were truly awesome and magnificent. Yet, as I looked down at the canyon, the Lord brought this passage from Proverbs 8 to mind.

This truth by comparison makes the Grand Canyon look like the small stream that flows through my backyard. There is nothing in this world that can compare to the wonder of the sacrificial love of the Son of God. To think that He would look on us in our sinful state, polluted by the stench of sin, and reach out and embrace us in His arms of grace and forgiveness. And then to say, "My delights were with the sons of men!" The Creator Himself saying that! Unfathomable love!

"Now therefore hearken unto me, O ye children: for blessed are they that keep My ways. Hear instruction, and be wise, and refuse it not. Blessed is the man that heareth Me, watching daily at My gates, waiting at the posts of My doors. For whoso findeth Me findeth life, and shall obtain favor of the Lord. But he that sinneth against Me wrongeth his own soul; all they that hate Me love death" (8:32-36).

Many things in life are not really all that important. If you miss them, it doesn't really matter. I remember running down a long concourse in Chicago's O'Hare Airport to catch a plane for Denver. I got there just as the gate closed and the plane was pulling out. But it didn't really matter. I went back to the ticket counter, changed my reservation, and caught a plane that was leaving a few minutes later, and was soon on my way.

Other things, however, are crucial, and if you miss them you could be in big trouble. If you forget to take your medicine, it could endanger your health. If you fail to show up at church on your wedding day, it could damage your future relationship and happiness with your spouse-to-be. This passage presents us with a crucial issue that we must not miss. It is given both positively and negatively. After all the great discourse on wisdom, the passage begins with, "Now therefore hearken unto Me." The positive statement is that we are to keep the ways of God (Prov. 8:32); the negative one is that "he that sinneth against Me wrongeth his own soul" (8:36).

In this case, to sin is to miss the mark. In contrast to the one who *"findeth* me findeth life," the one who *misses* does not. Great happiness and joy are in store for those who find wisdom and life, while great tragedy awaits those who do not. This is the issue of life and death.

The person who finds God is the eager learner who seeks Him. Such a person is watching daily at wisdom's gate, waiting at the posts of wisdom's doors. When there is something to be learned, he is right there. He is the type that is always on time for worship, for Bible study, for prayer meeting, and is there each morning to meet individually with God.

I was having a physical problem and went in for my examination. Lab tests were made, and then I waited for the results. I was *so* eager to find out what they were. I could hardly wait to hear the doctor's report. When he said, "You're in good shape," I was elated. I had really wanted to know. That's the attitude commended in this passage. Not the person with a casual take-it-or-leave-it attitude, but the one who is on the edge of his chair, waiting for wisdom to speak.

Another important truth comes through in this passage. Jesus Christ, the wisdom of God, has the happiness of His people on His heart. So He thoroughly enjoys teaching us His truth. That is important. You may have had a teacher who loved to teach. It shows clearly. The teacher who is there because he has to be does not usually do as good a job of teaching as the one who enjoys his work and *wants* to teach.

Jesus Christ *wants* to teach us. He has made every provision for us. So often it is not Satan or sin that hurts us, but we who hurt ourselves. We, in effect, "wrong our own selves." The application is clear, "Blessed are they that keep my ways" (Prov. 8:32).

So we have happiness on one hand and tragedy on the other. When we are in contempt of Christ and contradict His will and way in our lives, we have chosen the path of death. We have chosen to love that which will be the death of us and have pushed from us the only source of life. That is why God says through His prophet, "Incline your ear and come unto Me: hear and your soul shall live" (Isa. 55:3). Here wisdom has given us the means of life.

12

Contrast of Wisdom and Foolishness

Proverbs 9:1-18

A few years ago I was with a friend in Honolulu. We were down on Waikiki Beach early one morning looking for a place to eat breakfast. We saw a small restaurant in the International Market Place, so we went in. I had no idea what was in store for us when we entered. We went through the cafeteria line and I chose biscuits and eggs. We sat down at a table in the open air near the sidewalk, asked God's blessing on the food, and began to eat. I took a bite of one of the biscuits, and I was immediately transported by memories back to my childhood on the farm in Iowa. I had not tasted anything like it since I left home. It was absolutely delicious.

In 1976 my wife and I were on our way to the Orient for a six-month ministry assignment. We stopped in Honolulu where Virginia was to have some meetings with women's groups and I was to speak to servicemen. I chose our hotel near that restaurant. Early on our first morning there, we were on the street heading for breakfast. We arrived 30 minutes before the place opened, so we walked up and down the block looking at all the sights. Promptly at 8:00 A.M. they opened and we went in. I ordered biscuits, sat down, buttered them, and took a bite. There it was again, the same delicious flavor of days gone by.

Nothing calls your attention to this restaurant. It is neither fancy nor expensive. But when you taste the biscuits, you are in a different world. I've often thought that if I owned that restaurant, I'd be out on Kalakaua Avenue encouraging people to come in and dine. I'd tell them of the wonderful food that was being served. But I don't suppose too many people would believe me. They would probably continue to turn into the large, glamorous, expensive hotels and their dining rooms. They would think my claims were too good to be true.

The first part of the Book of Proverbs concludes with a continuation of the theme of praising the wisdom of God for what it is. Chapters 8 and 9 are a unit; the first part (chap. 8) personifies wisdom, while the second part (chap. 9) comes full circle with the overall theme in the first part of the book by contrasting the way of wisdom and the way of foolishness.

The chapter also ties together all the subthemes mentioned in the previous eight chapters. The chapter has three parts: the celebration of wisdom (9:1-6), contrasted with the celebration of foolishness (9:13-18); in the middle is the final invitation to following wisdom (9:7-12). This section again shows the contrast between the wise man and the scorner, with the key being in verse 10, "The fear of the Lord is the beginning of wisdom: and the knowledge of the holy is understanding."

"Wisdom hath builded her house, she hath hewn out her seven pillars: she hath killed her beasts; she hath mingled her wine; she hath also furnished her table. She hath sent forth her maidens: she crieth upon the highest places of the city, 'Whoso is simple, let him turn in hither;' as for him that wanteth understanding, she saith to him, 'Come, eat of my bread, and drink of the wine which I have mingled. Forsake the foolish, and live; and go in the way of understanding' " (9:1-6).

In this passage wisdom is portrayed as a magnificent queen who sends out her maidens to invite whosoever will to a sumptuous feast and celebration. The sacrifice has been offered, and all is in readiness. Anyone may enter and enjoy the feast.

The true feast that wisdom offers is spiritual. Here men can find their directions amid the many influences, pressures, and false teachings that abound in the world. Here directions are not couched in difficult and mysterious phrases. "Forsake the foolish, and live" is the admonition. It is a call that anyone can understand and follow.

The question is, of course, why so few do enter. One reason is because the call is so plain and clear. It is the nature of man to want to complicate things. Another reason is because it simply seems too good to be true. So few can bring themselves to believe that if they simply "turn in hither" they will find a sumptuous feast waiting for them. That is almost beyond description. And it's all free.

Christ has already made the sacrifice necessary for sin. Redemption and eternal life have been secured. Those of us who have experienced the fullness of the blessings of Christ are sent out to invite others. With wisdom we are to cry from the highest places in the city. We are to call all men to come and enjoy the feast of the wisdom of God (Isa. 55:1-3; Luke 14:15-24).

"He that reproveth a scorner getteth to himself shame: and he that rebuketh a wicked man getteth himself a blot. Reprove not a scorner, lest he hate thee: rebuke a wise man, and he will love thee. Give instruction to a wise man, and he will be yet wiser: teach a just man, and he will increase in learning. The fear of the Lord is the beginning of wisdom: and the knowledge of the holy is understanding. For by me thy days shall be multiplied, and the years of thy life shall be increased. If thou be wise, thou shalt be wise for thyself: but if thou scornest, thou alone shall bear it" (9:7-12).

If you already know it all, you cannot learn any more. That's true with anything. It is true in education, in spiritual matters, in sports. I watched with keen interest as Fred Wevodau taught my son Randy how to play tennis. Hour after hour they hit the ball back and forth, punctuated with periodic questions from Randy or admonitions from Fred. That fall Randy decided to try out for the tennis team. The coach watched his performance and then made some suggestions. Randy's response was most interesting. He could have said, "I already know all that." But he didn't. When the coach spoke, he listened. Even though he may have heard some of these instructions before or they may have been slightly different from what Fred had taught him, he thanked the coach and tried to apply them to his game. He made the team.

I doubt if Randy would have made the team if he had contradicted the coach or acted as if he knew it all. Attitude makes all the difference in the world in the learning process. The scorner and the person who is teachable are at the opposite ends of the spectrum. And here is the frightening thing: since wisdom *begins* with the fear of the Lord, the "know-it-all" cannot learn. He can never learn. He is doomed to remain in his self-imposed ignorance. He has locked the door of learning and thrown away the key.

The wise man is just the opposite. His spiritual radar is constantly tuned in to the source of wisdom, the Word of God. He approaches it with an open mind and an eager spirit. He knows his own limitations. He realizes his need for help. He understands his lack of true spiritual depth and so desires to go deeper into the truths of God's Word. The more he knows, the more he realizes there is yet more to know. He knows he can never arrive.

A friend of mine tells of meeting a lady in her 90s. Her first words to him were, "What have you been learning lately?" She had not leveled off; she was still reaching out. But scoffers and wicked men have made their choices. They are adversaries of the wisdom of God and have nothing to learn.

All too often they are witty, clever people who can make the person who reproves them look ridiculous. With a smirk and a smile they mock the truth of God. By their clever conversation they can phrase their words so that the way of God appears wrong and the way of the devil seems right. Remember that Satan has been a deceiver from the beginning.

When King Hezekiah sent messengers from city to city to invite the people to turn back to God to keep the Passover unto the Lord, the record says, "They laughed them to scorn and mocked them" (2 Chron. 30:10).

During His ministry, Jesus told of the king whose son was being married and who invited one and all to the feast. "The kingdom of heaven is like unto a certain king, which made a marriage for his son, and sent forth his servants to call them that were bidden to the wedding: and they would not come. Again, he sent forth other servants, saying, 'Tell them which are bidden, "Behold, I have prepared my dinner; my oxen and my fatlings are killed, and all things are ready; come unto the marriage" ' " (Matt. 22:2-4). But "they made light of it and went their ways" (22:5).

So we are to stay out of the scorner's chair and also to stay away from the scorner. Instead, be a wise man and work with wise men, for in this way all will be the wiser and all will increase in their learning.

In the last part of this passage we have two tremendous truths set before us. There appears to be a link between godly living and physical health, and most of us have heard physicians in recent years talk about this. A peaceful mind and spirit contribute to lower doctor bills, fewer aspirins and ulcers, and less time in the clinics and hospitals.

The second truth about individual responsibility is a bit harder to apprehend. We are responsible for our own acts. If we act in accord with the wisdom of God, it will be to our benefit. On the other hand, if we live in contempt of the law of God, we will pay the penalty. Amazing words in a day and age when no one wants to be responsible for anything. It is always the fault of the other person, our world says. I can blame my parents, my home life, my environment, my education or lack of it, anything, as long as I'm not held responsible for the sins I have committed and the problems I have gotten myself into.

But the facts are that what we are and what we become are the fruit of our own decisions and personal choices. We must bear the responsibility for our individual destinies. Dawson Trotman, founder of the Navigators, used to tell us:

"Sow a thought, and reap a word;
sow a word, and reap an act;
sow an act, and reap a habit;
sow a habit, and reap a character;
sow a character, and reap a destiny."

The Apostle Paul stated, "Be not deceived; God is not mocked: for whatsoever a man soweth, that shall he also reap" (Gal. 6:7). The Old Testament prophet put it this way: "The soul that sinneth, it shall die. The son shall not bear the iniquity of the father, neither shall the father bear the iniquity of the son: the righteousness of the righteous shall be upon him, and the wickedness of the wicked shall be upon him" (Ezek. 18:20).

Satan can tempt, but he cannot force us to sin. Wicked companions can lure us into the wrong paths, but they are only the devil's instruments and cannot force us to follow their ways. Ultimately each one of us is responsible for his own individual acts.

These things may sound strange to those who have been fed the philosophy of the day and have swallowed it whole. But the Bible teaches that truth from beginning to end. Let's go back to the beginning. Adam had a perfect Father; he had a perfect home; he had a perfect environment. When he chose to do evil, whom could he blame? His Father? No, for God does not tempt us to sin. His home life? No, for God did nothing during His and Adam's communion together in Eden that could have led Adam to rebellion. His environment? No, for it was perfect.

The fact is that he *chose* to rebel against God. He made the decision and God held him responsible for it. Naturally in His great love there was forgiveness based on the provision made in the "Seed" (the Saviour to come), but Adam sinned and was held accountable. Fellowship would be restored, but punishment would be meted out. As Solomon says in this passage, "If thou scornest, thou alone shall bear it" (Prov. 9:12). Powerful and truthful words! Words we need to hear today.

We must be alert in this life to seek the will of God and then do it. Let our one desire be to please Him and bring joy to His heart. And let it come, not from a sense of duty, but from a sense of gratitude for His grace, mercy, and love; for His salvation offered full and free; and for all the benefits with which He blesses us daily.

"A foolish woman is clamorous: she is simple, and knoweth nothing. For she sitteth at the door of her house, on a seat in the high places of the city, to call passengers who go right on their ways: 'Whoso is simple, let him turn in hither: and as for him that wanteth understanding,' she saith to him, 'Stolen waters are sweet, and bread eaten in secret is pleasant.' But he knoweth not that the dead are there; and that her guests are in the depths of hell" (9:13-18).

When I was a kid, our local movie theaters would occasionally show a Jimmy Cagney movie. It was usually a fairly simple plot. Cagney would play the part of a tough young kid, raised in a rough part of town, growing up on the wrong side of the law. Pat O'Brian would play a tough Irish cop who eventually had to catch him and put him in jail. If the crime had been especially violent, he would wind up in solitary and be put on a ration of bread and water.

That's the part that would get to me. I grew up on an Iowa farm where we had plenty of fresh milk, eggs, homemade jam, and fresh vegetables. We would butcher our own meat, so we ate very well. I remember wondering how a person could survive on only bread and water. Such a diet seemed to be the ultimate in discomfort and punishment.

In this passage we are introduced to a pathetic sight. First we were introduced to wisdom and the sumptuous feast she offered. But here we meet a foolish, clamorous, and ignorant woman who is holding her offer of bread and water—her "feast"—to those who pass by. She has prepared a banquet of stolen water and the bread of death. The contrast is vivid and the climax is shattering.

On one side you have wisdom calling, "Let the simple turn to me. You will find the way of life and understanding." On the opposite side you have the foolish woman, holding out an offer of death and hell, also calling, "Whoso is simple, let him turn in hither." The contrast is plain. You can eat a gracious feast or sup on bread and water. Now who in his right mind would prefer bread and water to a full banquet? The answer is astounding. Most people do!

The majority of people on this earth reject the wisdom of God and prefer the husks and pollution of sin. The devil has a large following. Why is that? First, because the pathetic reality of sin is often glossed over with a thin coating of glamour and the false promise of happiness. The snares of debauchery and empty pleasure appear more exciting than the more lasting and satisfying blessings offered by the wisdom of God.

Second, we are all intrigued by that which is forbidden. This is the heritage left us by Adam and Eve, who lusted after the forbidden fruit simply because it was forbidden. All the trees were good to look on, but this one was out-of-bounds. So they wanted it.

Such foolish desire is a mark of the human race. Tell a child he cannot do something and immediately he wants to do it. Tell people they cannot read a certain book and immediately they want to read it. We like to go beyond the boundaries that have been set for us. We know the highway of God is safe, but we prefer to travel the treacherous road of sin. The major question men should ask is, "Where does that road lead?" The answer is that it leads to death and hell.

So the first part of the Book of Proverbs ends with a climactic appeal, reminding the reader that the way of God is full and satisfying, while the way of the devil is full of disappointments and ends in tragedy—in death and hell.

It is appropriate to end this examination of Solomon's sage advice with a contrast of the way of wisdom with the way of scorners, throwing out the same challenge Joshua did at the end of his life: "Choose you this day whom ye will serve!" May God enable all of us to answer with that valiant leader, "As for me and my house, we will serve the Lord!" (Josh. 24:15)

Inspirational Victor Books for Your Enjoyment

HOW GOD CAN USE NOBODIES A study, by James Montgomery Boice, of the lives of Abraham, Moses, and David—Old Testament men who were small enough to be great. Textbook **6-2027—$1.75**/Leader's Guide **6-2922—95¢**

WHAT WORKS WHEN LIFE DOESN'T? What works when happiness eludes you? You face discouragement? In 12 selected Psalms, Stuart Briscoe stays close to the biblical text, yet uses contemporary anecdotes and relevant applications for a very practical study that answers these questions and more. Textbook **6-2725—$1.95**/Leader's Guide (with transparency masters) **6-2946—$1.95**

BE FREE An expository study of Galatians by Warren W. Wiersbe. Challenges the Christian to recognize and live according to the true freedom he has in Christ. Leader's Guide includes overhead projector masters, with instructions for making transparencies. Textbook **6-2716 —$1.95**/Leader's Guide **6-2938—$1.95**

KNOW THE MARKS OF CULTS Dave Breese exposes common and characteristic errors of all cults. Sounds a warning and a note of encouragement to true believers. Textbook **6-2704—$1.75**/Leader's Guide **6-2917—95¢**

THE FRAGRANCE OF BEAUTY Scripturally based study, by Joyce Landorf, on wrong attitudes that mar a woman's beauty—and help for correcting them. Textbook **6-2231—$1.75**/Leader's Guide **6-2912—$1.25**

24 WAYS TO IMPROVE YOUR TEACHING Dr. Kenneth Gangel, experienced Christian educator, describes 24 teaching methods, and gives concrete suggestions for using them in teaching the Word of God. Leader's Guide includes overhead projector masters, with instructions for making transparencies. Textbook **6-2463—$2.25**/Leader's Guide **6-2927—$1.95**

THE COMPLETE CHRISTIAN Larry Richards gives insights for life from the Book of Hebrews. Emphasizes reaching spiritual maturity thru steady growth and faith. Leader's Guide includes overhead projector masters, with instructions for making transparencies. Textbook **6-2714 —$1.95**/Leader's Guide **6-2937—$1.95**

WHAT HAPPENS WHEN WOMEN PRAY Evelyn Christenson, with Viola Blake, deals with methods and spiritual principles of prayer. Inspirational and practical. Textbook **6-2715—$1.95**/Leader's Guide **6-2943 —$1.25**

DISCIPLES ARE MADE—NOT BORN Walt Henrichsen, personnel director worldwide for The Navigators, discusses what discipleship is and the training of a disciple. Textbook **6-2706—$1.95**/Leader's Guide **6-2919—95¢**

Add 40¢ postage and handling for the first book, and 10¢ for each additional title. Add $1 for minimum order service charge for orders less than $5.

Prices are subject to change without notice.

VICTOR BOOKS

Buy these titles at your local Christian bookstore or order from a division of SP Publications, Inc.
WHEATON, ILLINOIS 60187

A